OCD: Hiding in Plain Sight

Andrea Brown

OCD: Hiding in Plain Sight
Published through Firewalker Publishing
www.firewalkerpublishing.com

All rights reserved
Copyright © 2023 by Andrea Brown
Cover art Copyright @ 2023 by Andrea Brown

Primary Editor – Ashley Kellis
Final Editing – Barbara Spencer and John Martin Sr.

ISBN: 987-0-98927219-3-6 (Paperback Edition)
ISBN: 987-0-98927219-4-3 (E-Book Edition)

No part of this publication may be reproduced, stored in a retrieval system, or transmitted in any form or by any means electronic, mechanical, photocopying, recording, or otherwise, without the written permission of the author or publisher.

Some names have been changed in this book to protect and be protected.

Table of Contents

Introduction 1

Chapter 1 3

Chapter 2 19

Chapter 3 37

Chapter 4 55

Chapter 5 71

Chapter 6 89

Chapter 7 109

Chapter 8 123

Chapter 9 139

Chapter 10 157

Chapter 11 169

Chapter 12 181

Conclusion 193

Dedication

To my husband Cody,
for being the first person to make me feel safe.

Introduction

From the outside, I look like a high functioning, successful girl in my twenties. I grew up in a small town with two loving parents. I graduated college in three years with a bachelor's in social work. When I was twenty, I started dating my best friend and I knew he was going to be my husband from the first time we kissed. We bought a house a few months before we got married. We both had good jobs that we enjoyed and paid well. Everything seemed normal on the outside. No one knew what was really going on inside my head.

My first memory as a child is lying in bed telling myself not to move or else the person hiding in the closet was going to come out and kill me. Anytime I was home alone, I wouldn't allow myself to move from a certain spot on the couch or else I would be kidnapped. In college I once checked the microwave to see if someone was hiding inside it because I was too scared to sleep without doing so. What's the catch? No one has ever been in my house or tried to hurt me in any way. It was all in my head. Every day for nearly twenty years, my mind told me I was going to be raped then killed. It was my destiny.

* * *

OCD: Hiding in Plain Sight is my story of what it was like living with a severe mental illness while being able to portray I was 'normal.' No one knew how scared I was all the time. No one knew the dark, violent thoughts I had no matter what situation I was in. At the age of twenty-four, I finally received the answer I didn't know I was looking for: obsessive compulsive disorder (OCD).

OCD is commonly misunderstood and lessens the likelihood of those who suffer to be properly diagnosed. It's common to take 15+ years from onset of symptoms to diagnosis. My story is not an uncommon one. My hope is by using my real time journal and thought log entries, readers will understand the fear this illness can cause and spread awareness to help others.

Chapter 1

"Andrea, I don't want you to freak out, but I think you have OCD." It's the end of the session and I'm sitting across from my therapist, Wanda, trying to comprehend what she just said. I feel my eyes gloss over and my jaw drops. I stop playing with the fidget toy I have in my hand. All I can hear is the white noise machine she has in her office. *Is she joking?* OCD has never come up during my past year of therapy.

"Wait, OCD as in obsessive compulsive disorder? I don't have that."

"Remember last week you mentioned some checking you were doing because of how paranoid you get? That can be a form of OCD."

I think back to last week's session. Towards the end of the session, I was in a good mood and started joking about seeing some pictures online depicting a "paranoid parrot." There were tons of pictures of things people do when they are paranoid, and

I told her that I could relate. I told her how I would check to make sure I put my debit card back in my wallet multiple times after I pump gas because I always think it has been moved and if I lose it, then it would be all my fault. She seemed interested at the time, so I also told her about how I would lock a door then turn back around a few times to make sure it was still locked. Looking back, I remember the look she gave me after I talked about my checking tendencies. I didn't realize it then, but that's when everything clicked for her.

Wanda continues, pulling me out of my thoughts, "I want you to read these descriptions about anxiety and OCD to see what you think." I reach out to grab the two sheets of paper she has but instead it feels like I'm grabbing a book full of reasons why I'm crazy. "Let's schedule a session on Tuesday, and we can discuss it to see which one feels like the right fit."

Walking out of the office, I feel like everything has changed. The front desk staff catches me off guard, "hey Andrea, have a great weekend!"

I mutter back all I can, "yeah, you too." I continue what feels like a walk of shame.

How is this possible? Lately I've been feeling better and like I am finally learning how to handle myself. I've been doing all my coping skills just like Wanda has told me to do! I haven't had panic attacks in months because I'm doing all I can to manage my anxiety. Besides, isn't OCD when people close doors or clean a lot? I have a flashback of the TV show I remember watching as a kid. There were three people with OCD. One person would open and close doors repeatedly until it felt right. The next person hoarded cats, then would obsessively clean to keep up with the consequences of having so many cats. The last person used a counting method to figure out what items she could get at the store. I'm not like that. I do none of those things so how could I possibly be diagnosed with OCD?

I pull myself back to focus on what to do next. I need a minute alone. Walking into the bathroom, I throw everything on the counter and take some deep breaths as I stare at the ground. Slowly I look up into the mirror but can't recognize who I am anymore. Every negative thought I've ever had about myself feels like it has been confirmed. *You're a failure. You've always been crazy and nothing you do can ever save you. Everyone laughs at you for how scared you always are, and you deserve it. You'll be scared for the rest of your life because that's all you deserve.* Looking down at the papers Wanda gave me to read, all I want is to rip them up and ignore the session ever happened. After five minutes, I finally collect myself and decide to leave the bathroom to face reality. Walking to my car, each step becomes slower as it feels like the weight of the world just landed on my back. All I can feel is disgust in myself. *I knew you were crazy* swirls around in my head the whole drive back to my office.

As I drive to work, I try to pull myself together. My job is full of social workers and all we do is talk about mental health and our emotions. We do feelings check-ins twice a day, so there's no way I can go in with my mind in a funk. I plaster a smile on my face and say hi to every employee I pass on the way to my desk. I could easily find someone to talk to about all this, but I just want to bury all the fear, confusion, and sadness. The only thing I can think of doing is getting organized. My office has three other people in it, but I'm usually the one to do the organizing every few months. If the office ever looks messy or disorganized, I take on the responsibility, or else I can't forgive myself.

First, I pull out all our craft supplies. I already have a system in place, but this new one will be better. This time I'll wrap the boxes in construction paper, so they look better from a distance. The storage unit only faces my desk, but I can see it and it's not good enough. I can feel my coworker, Alex, looking at me as I start to measure the construction paper to the boxes "you know that it's pointless to do that, right?"

I barely look up as I respond, "I know, but it will look better this way. I can't stand seeing it looking all messy the old way."

"It was fine the old way. Plus, we're the only ones that use those supplies."

I laugh off her comments and chop it up to being a "me" thing to do. Everyone in my office knows how I am.

After I finish covering all the boxes and putting the supplies in the appropriate places, I start on the bookshelf. I cannot even count how many times I have reorganized it, but I know it can be better. I pull all the books off to reorder them, so they'll look more appealing. There are some books that have useful information, so I go to the copier to start scanning pages to my computer for electronic copies. Deep down though, I know I'll never look at them again, but this way I'll have more resources. In case anyone ever needs anything, I'll be prepared. I'll be praised for how prepared and useful I am.

I ran into my coworker, Julie, in the copy room. She asks me about a client I have. "Hey Andrea, how's it going with Doug?"

"Oh good. I'm supposed to meet with him in a couple weeks. I'm finally starting to get somewhere with him by just listening and letting him take the lead. I'm hoping he'll start to agree to other services soon, like therapy and medications."

"I like the idea of letting him feel some control. That's probably what he needs right now. Why is he so resistant to other services?"

"I'm not sure. I think he just doesn't believe he needs them."

"He may be so used to living in crisis mode all the time that he doesn't know how to get ahead of it."

"Yeah, that's true. Maybe next time I meet with him, I can sit him down and figure out how to problem solve. Maybe that way we can figure out some of the bigger problems and I can help him figure them out. Plus, he may be more open to talk to me if I'm taking on some of the things he needs help with."

"That's a great idea. Good job!"

By the time Julie leaves, I've scanned around fifty worksheets to my computer and decide that it's enough. I walk back to my office repeating the whole conversation repeatedly in my head. I start separating the scanned copies into folders on my computer and I start repeating the phrase "that's a great idea" in my head. I start to move my toes and pretend to type the phrase out on an imaginary keyboard. "That's a great idea. That's a great idea. That's a great idea."

Suddenly, Alex interrupts me "hey do you know of any sport programs that are going on right now?"

I respond, "No but let me look."

"Oh no it's okay. I was just wondering. I'm sure I'll find something eventually." Instead of forgetting about it, I drop everything and spend the next thirty minutes looking. I have gathered up a list of five resources that could provide the services Alex is looking for. I list the websites, cost, age ranges, location and registration deadlines. Before sending it to her, I go back to the websites and double check all the information. Did I make any mistakes? What if I entered the wrong deadline and her client doesn't get signed up? I go back to the websites and double check all the information. Finally, it feels ready.

"Okay, I'm sending you a few different resources now." I wait to see Alex's reaction.

"Cool, thanks."

Oh no, she hates it. I didn't do it good enough and now she's mad that I found them without her asking. I need to fix it. "Hey, I have some extra time today. Do you want me to organize some of the papers that you have scattered around your desk?" I ask Alex in hopes of making sure she's not upset with me.

"Really? Yeah, that'd be awesome if you had some extra time. Just organize it however you think works best."

I grab all the papers and start sorting. The disorganization makes me feel uneasy and I know I must fix it. How is a worksheet about making a safety plan with a random flier for food assistance? This list of therapists is useless if it's going to be in this random pile! How can she work like this? I pull open my drawer to see all the folders I have that are labeled and utilized to their fullest. In order to figure out how to organize Alex's papers, I need to reference mine, so I start to pull the folders out of the drawer to go through them. Wait, why do I have all these things together instead of in separate folders like they should be? I push Alex's things to the side while I start to reorganize my own mess. A new system is needed. A better system.

An hour later, I finally have my desk and Alex's desk organized. I return to look at the resources I had sent to her an hour earlier to review it again. Did I make a mistake? Hopefully she'll look at the website herself so I'm not to blame if something goes wrong. The books from the shelf are all over the floor still. I grab them to put them in a new order. A better order.

My checking and organization never stopped throughout the day. I continued to move things around and work to make better systems for everything. Different resources I've made were checked and emails were re-read, just to make sure I made no mistakes. "That's a great idea" was typed out by my toes more times than I'd like to admit. All the while, OCD swirled around my head. I wanted to read the descriptions I was given this morning, but each time I started to pull them out of my bag, I shoved them back in. I wasn't ready to know.

Walking in the house I hear my husband, Cody, playing video games. I start to think about how grateful I am for him. We met when we were sixteen, instantly becoming best friends. I could confide in him about all my teenage insecurities, and he knew how to make me feel better. When we were friends, I saw how he treated his girlfriends and knew that's what I wanted. Every man I dated had to meet the standards that Cody had unknowingly set.

"Hey babe" I go in to give him a kiss then sit in the swivel chair on the opposite side of the living room.

"You look cute today babe" Cody says with a smile before going back to playing his game. I love it when he compliments my outfits.

I start to look around the room to look at all our pictures that we've taken over the years. To my right is the first picture we ever took together when we started dating. I was in college, and he was visiting me for the weekend in my dorm. After four years of being friends, he finally asked me to be his girlfriend that weekend. Next to it is a picture of us zip lining. Cody planned a mini vacation to Missouri a couple years ago but didn't tell me we were going zip lining on the last day. I had no clue until we pulled up and I saw the giant tower and asked, "do I have to jump off that thing cause that's not happening!" I turn to my left to see a picture from the first time we went to Grand Cayman. We were snorkeling in the ocean when Cody wanted to try to take a picture with a waterproof camera. The picture cut off half our foreheads and you could tell we were trying to smile even with the snorkels in our mouths. During that trip I was stung by a jellyfish during a jet ski tour and the instructor asked me "you mind if he pees on you?" pointing to Cody. Apparently, urine helps lessen the pain of a jellyfish sting, but there was no way that was happening. I told him that I'd just deal with the pain without any urine. Later that night, he proposed so I'm grateful our proposal story doesn't start with "well he had to pee on me earlier in the day." On the wall by the TV is one of our wedding pictures. We're walking on the grass next to a pond, holding hands while I'm looking at Cody with the biggest smile on my face. I can't help but look down at my wedding ring and remember everything we've been through together as a couple. Cody has always been there, no matter what. My smile starts to fade when I remember the other side of all the pictures. I remember all the fear and anxiety that accompanied each of the events. That weekend in the dorm, I didn't want Cody to ask me out because I didn't think I was good enough for him. During snorkeling, it was a fact in my mind that I was going to be severely hurt because the ocean was too dangerous. When we were ziplining, each time the instructors told me to step off the ledge to zip line, I couldn't help but make scenarios about the rope breaking. During our wedding, I had just started medication that took away the anxiety, but also made me feel little to no emotions. Each memory has its positives. The parts that we tell everyone when they ask about the pictures, but no one knows the other side. No one knows how much fear I constantly have. I don't even understand why I've always had that fear but it's something I remember having since I was a little kid. I look down at the description of OCD and wonder, am I about to find out why?

I turn my attention back to Cody, grateful that I'm able to spend my life with him, but terrified he won't want to be with me if I'm diagnosed with OCD. He's already done so much to try to understand my constant paranoia. Is this going to be too much to handle?

Finally, I work up the courage to say what I've been avoiding all day "So Wanda thinks I have OCD."

Cody looks at me, shrugs his shoulders and says, "I don't think so."

Good, Cody doesn't think I'm crazy so maybe that means I'm okay. "Yeah, I don't think so either but she's having me read about it and see how it feels once I read the descriptions for anxiety and OCD."

I flip back and forth between which one I want to read first. I decide to start with the Generalized Anxiety Disorder description first. It's been my diagnosis for the past year and what I've been working to treat this whole time. It must be the right one.

"Generalized Anxiety Disorder involves constant and chronic worrying, nervousness and tension. Instead of the fear being connected to a certain situation or thing, it is a general feeling of dread."

Yes, that's what I have. I'm always worried about things. I knew nothing was wrong with me. Now let's get it over with and read about OCD.

"Obsessive Compulsive Disorder: Obsessions are thoughts, images or impulses that occur repeatedly that trigger distressing feelings. Compulsions are behaviors individuals do to get rid of the obsessions and/or decrease the anxiety."

Wait, is this what Wanda was talking about when she mentioned my paranoia?

"In most cases, people with OCD realize that the obsessions don't make any sense. They usually cause feelings such as fear or a feeling that things must be done "just right." Obsessions can be time consuming and get in the way of important activities."

No, this isn't happening. Am I reading this right?

"Compulsions are repetitive behaviors or thoughts to neutralize obsessions; however, it's generally only a temporary solution. Examples can include checking, cleaning and getting reassurance."

The pages become blurry as my eyes start to tear up. "It's true, I have OCD" I say to Cody in almost a whisper. I continue to hold the paper up as my eyes bolt back and forth trying to comprehend what's happening. Cody stops his game and comes over to kneel in front of me, placing his hands on my knees. I barely notice he moved but continue to talk in a whisper. "All the paranoia I've had my entire life, it's actually been OCD." I re-read the descriptions over and over to see if I'm misunderstanding somehow.

"How is that OCD?" Cody asks with a concerned, yet nonjudgement tone.

"I check things all the time! I am always checking the locks and checking around me. At night when we're lying in bed, I'm always looking behind me to make sure no one is standing there. Do you know how many times I check the locks before we go to bed?" The tears start to fall as Cody climbs into the chair with me to hold me. "How can this be true? How did no one notice for so long?"

It feels like eternity that I'm crying on Cody's shoulder. All the while my brain repeats all the bad things that it said when I was leaving Wanda's office. *You're a failure. You've always been crazy and nothing you do can ever save you. Everyone laughs at you for how scared you always are, and you deserve it. You'll be scared for the rest of your life because that's all you deserve. Cody won't love you anymore once he finds out how crazy you really are.* The thoughts are right. I need to show Cody that I'm strong. The tears start to slow down when Cody asks, "Is there anything I can do to help?"

"Just keep being you" I say with a half-smile. I don't want him to be upset. He's always appearing so strong, and I don't want to make things any harder for him.

Throughout the night, I do my best to stay distracted. I watch TV shows, play games on my phone and talk with Cody about anything in order to avoid thinking about OCD. It starts to get darker out, so just like usual, my paranoia increases. When it's time to go to bed, I lock the patio door while Cody heads to the bedroom. I make it to the light switch in the living room and notice he hasn't turned the light on in the bedroom yet. I ask, "Can you turn that light on so I can turn this light off?"

His head pops around the doorway, "Just walk over here."

My mind begins to panic. I can't walk in the dark, something bad will happen. Even though he's standing right there, Cody may not be able to save me from whoever is going to hurt me once all the lights are out. The only time I can be in the dark is when we're both in bed for the night. "No, can you just please turn on the bedroom light? I don't want to be in the dark."

"I'm right here though."

"I know" I hang my head "I can't really explain it, just please turn it on, okay?"

He gives in and turns on the light. Once again, I feel like I'm doing a walk of shame to the bedroom as my brain tells me I'm pathetic for not being able to walk in the dark. I go into the bedroom, close the door and make sure to lock it. Going into the bathroom, I do a quick check behind the door and behind the shower door. Brushing my teeth, I avoid looking into the mirror because if I do, then someone may appear behind me. I only use the mirror when I'm going to the bathroom because behind the toilet is a window that I'm always fearful someone is going to come through to choke me. After finishing up in the bathroom, I walk to the bed but first do a visual check that the bedroom door is still locked before laying down.

I start to reach up to the light to turn it off when Cody speaks up, "Baby, did you journal?"

"I don't want to journal tonight, I'm too tired." I groan, even though I know I need to write about my day since it's one of few ways to calm my anxiety.

"You asked me to hold you accountable and make sure you do it every night."

"I know and I appreciate you doing it. It just sucks sometimes." I reluctantly grab my journal knowing I'm not ready to express my true feelings just yet. Every word from the description about OCD spins around my mind as I start to write.

Journal Entry: Well, I have OCD. Reading through the descriptions really helped me understand what I do and why. It all kind of makes sense now. I'm not alone. Part of me is excited to have an answer, but the other part is terrified. Am I finally going to get help after all these years? It sucks that I'll have a different diagnosis, but that's okay. I have my support and will work through it to get better. I know I can.

I quickly close my journal without reading what I wrote. I don't have to see Wanda for a couple more days, so until then, I can act like everything is normal. Sitting up, I reach to turn the light off, but first check to make sure the bedroom door is still locked. Laying down, the words start to repeat themselves as I start typing with my toes, making it hard to sleep "I have OCD. I have OCD. I have OCD."

Chapter 2

It's finally Tuesday. I've been doing my best to make it the past four days without thinking about the fact that I'm about to be diagnosed with OCD. Sitting in the waiting room, waiting for Wanda to call me into her office, I feel like I'm going to be sick. My anxiety is taking over and the butterflies in my stomach feel like their wings are knives poking me in the stomach. There is a bin of stuffed animals that I'm tempted to climb into. Maybe if I'm covered in their softness, everything will feel okay. Or I can just run away. Maybe I can just do something stupid enough that will make it so I never have to come back here. That way, I'll never truly know if my diagnosis is OCD because Wanda hasn't confirmed it yet.

Wanda walks out with a smile on her face. I give half a smile back then walk into Wanda's office knowing that the words I was about to say would officially change my life, "You were right, I do have OCD."

Wanda gives me a warm, welcome smile "Okay, how did it feel to read the descriptions?"

"Part of me wanted to jump for joy that I finally had an answer about why I've been so scared and paranoid my whole life. The other part of me was scared because OCD feels so serious. Anxiety is so much more well-known and accepted. I feel like saying I have OCD is saying that I can't live a normal life and that people will treat me differently. They're going to expect me to be a germaphobe or something. It's something I don't know how to control." I put my head down in shame. "After I stopped crying when I realized how much the descriptions applied to me, I looked back at my life and realized so many moments that I was scared and did something to make it better. How did I not realize it? How did no one realize it?"

"Well in your case, we've talked about your paranoia before, but we hadn't talked about your compulsions until recently. We didn't know the routine you went through to make yourself feel safe."

"I just feel like my brain is broken."

"You're not broken."

I barely hear her due to my anger starting to build "Also I'm a social worker! I work with people that have mental health problems and I had no idea that I've been living with OCD for like twenty years. Are you kidding me? How am I supposed to be helping people if I can't even help myself?"

"It's not your fault. A lot of people don't realize they have OCD because not a lot of people know what it really is. Too often it's seen as a 'positive' diagnosis because people use it to describe just being organized. As you know, that's not all it is."

"I was one of those people! I had no clue how bad it is to live with until I started to think back. I've lived with it practically my whole freaking life!" All my childhood memories start to come back to me. "I remember lying in bed when I was elementary age and being terrified. I would lay in the middle covered up, lying like a statue because I thought if I moved then someone would get me. And whenever I was left home alone, I would always stay in one spot and never move. I would start to feel sick with how little I would eat or use the bathroom, but it didn't matter. Moving equaled getting killed by whoever had snuck into the house. Do you know how many times I got in trouble because I wouldn't do my chores? I never felt safe enough to walk around the house alone. Sometimes I would even lock myself out of the house on purpose because I was too scared to stay inside!" I drop my head into my hands. "I just can't believe this" *I'm so stupid for missing it for this long.*

"Andrea, did you ever have anyone break into your house or anything like that?"

I pop up my head "No! That's why it's never made any sense as to why I'm like this. Is it some type of repressed memory or something that I can't remember but I'm still reacting to? I've just never understood how people could just be at home alone or walk around in the dark. I've always been the odd man out." I push my hair back and try to sit up straight to try to gather myself. I don't want to be weak. I can handle this.

"It's common for people with OCD to worry about having some type of traumatic event happen to them or a repressed memory or something. This is what OCD does."

I start laughing to lighten the mood, "Well it sucks."

Wanda always sees past my walls, "Did you ever talk about your paranoia growing up?"

"Yeah, I would try to, but usually it was turned into a joke."

"Like how?"

"Well growing up my friends always knew I feared everything. They figured out I feared trees and honestly, I avoided them as much as I could, especially at night. I was worried that someone was going to jump out and hurt me. Eventually it somehow escalated to the person in the tree would have a frying pan. So, then it was just a huge joke that more and more people started to know about. I was the girl who feared a person hiding in a tree with a frying pan. Then one night I was at home and one of my friends called me asking to come hang out at the park across the street. They came over to my house so I could walk with them. When we got to the building that's at the park, one of them came running around the corner towards me with frying pans, screaming. I ran away, terrified that one of my nightmares was about to come true." I put my head down to hide the pain I was feeling from the memory. "Anytime something like that happened I felt like I was going to die."

"I'm sorry things like that happened."

I shrug my shoulders as it is something I have become used to. "I never wanted to go to my basement when I was a kid and honestly, I still never do now. It just feels like someone will be down there and will do whatever they can to hurt me. Even if I scream for help, no one will be able to hear me and I'm not strong enough to help myself. But growing up, I still would have to go to our basement to do laundry or grab something for my parents. Sometimes my siblings would even close the door and lock it from the outside. I would scream for help, but they'd leave me down there until my parents told them to knock it off. When they would let me out, they would tease me that I didn't just turn on the light. They didn't understand that my mind was in fight or flight mode. I had no ability to think rationally at that moment because I was convinced that I was about to be captured and killed. I never really told anyone though, so I don't blame any of them that laughed or made jokes about it. They were all innocent pranks or just things siblings do. Anyone else would be fine with them and be able to laugh them off. I'm the one that can't handle them."

There is a long silence before Wanda speaks up, "Let's try something so we can figure out what kind of thoughts you're having that's causing these types of reactions. I want you to start a log with the paranoid or irrational thoughts you have. Bring it back next week and we'll go over it."

Walking out of therapy my emotions feel out of sorts. How am I supposed to know if my thoughts are rational or irrational? I never know anymore! Right then a man comes walking toward me from the other end of the hallway. Immediately, I assess the situation as my panic grows. *Okay, he's going to try to grab me so he can assault me then kill me.* I keep my head down and after passing him, check behind to make sure he's not following me. When I drive back to my office, look around to make sure no one is following my car. Mid-plan, I stop on the stairwell and think about what just happened. *Was that an irrational thought? He was just a normal looking guy, who did nothing to me at all and I thought he was going to kill me.* It's then I start to realize how much trouble I'm in.

Knowing I will need help with this new homework assignment, I immediately approach Alex when I get back to work. Besides Cody, she is one of the few that I can talk to about everything.

"So, I found out today that I'm officially diagnosed with OCD. All that paranoia I've talked about that I have. Well, turns out those are my obsessions, and my compulsions revolve around checking." So far, she seems to be taking it well, so I continue, "I'm supposed to be creating a log for my irrational thoughts, but I never know what's irrational or not. Do you think you could be my irrational buddy and call me out when something I do or say is irrational?"

Alex smiles, "Of course. How do you want me to do it? Just tell you up front?"

"Yeah probably. Then I may have to ask how it's irrational so I can understand what's normal vs. not normal. I already need to add one to the list." I grab my phone to start a new note.

Thought Log:

Concerned about the man walking towards me, thought he was going to kill me.

Throughout the day, I realize there is no getting away from the thoughts. They are far more prevalent than I thought.

Thought Log:

Worried about constant headaches and neck pain. Completed a check online to verify health.

Worried about getting into a car accident and making a scenario about what would happen.

Worried about the person in the car next to me going to get out and grab me.

Made a scenario about getting shot as I walked to my car in the parking lot.

Worried when I opened the garage door to pull in, someone would be waiting on the other side waiting for me.

Moved the body pillow out from under the blanket on the bed to check to make sure it wasn't a person and to avoid the worry later.

After each entry, I feel more and more like a failure. Is there any way to get better if I'm this far gone? These are the types of thoughts I've had for years. I'm so used to them they don't seem bad until now that I write them out.

Thought Log:

Heard keys rattling and worried someone was breaking in. Knew it was likely Cody but couldn't shake the feeling it was someone else.

While showering, thinking someone was about to open the door and strangle me after killing Cody.

Heard a noise, thought someone was in the house ready to break through the bedroom door to hurt me.

The next morning, I read through my thought log. *How can I have this many violent and terrible thoughts in just one day? Have I always been like this? What in the world caused this to happen?* I snap back into reality and realize I can't think about that. I need to focus on how I am going to make it through the next week. Cody is going to be out of town for work and these are always the worst nights.

Throughout the day at work, all I can think about is having to be home alone that night. I contemplate how I can keep myself safe and what time I should get home for the best protection. If I go home later, is that safer or is it better to be inside the house before it gets dark? What if I go home and go straight to bed? If I go home and don't check every room, does that mean I'm less likely to be hurt? Is it better to find someone that's hiding in your house or avoid them?

I decide to work extra hours so I can spend less time at home, but still get home before it gets dark. I pull into the garage, knowing it's time to face fate. I exit through the big garage door so that I don't have to walk through the garage in the dark to get to the smaller door.

Thought Log:

When you open the house door, there will be someone standing on the other side waiting for you.

Once I get inside, the fear sets in that I always feel on these nights. The fear won't leave until I go to work tomorrow. My head starts to have the same thought that will revolve all night. *You won't make it out alive. You won't make it out alive. You won't make it out alive.* I have no hope of surviving, but I need to do what I can to protect myself. I lock the back door and set the alarm. I check the closet, then the hallway bathroom. As I walk towards the basement, I turn to make sure the back door is still locked, and the alarm is still set.

Thought Log:

What if someone is behind you and unlocked the door to let someone in?

I turn around again and walk back to make sure the alarm is still set. *Okay, it's still locked so I can keep going.* I push in the door stop into the basement door as far as it can go to check to make sure no one is down there.

Thought Log:

Has it been moved since this morning? What if someone is down there waiting while someone else put it back and is now hiding in the rest of the house?

I turn around to make sure the back door is still locked, and the doorstop hasn't moved since I pushed it in. Finally, the first hallway is checked. I tiptoe my way to the living room. I do a quick look over to make sure it's safe to enter. Behind the curtains? Clear. Behind the chair? Clear. Behind the couch? Clear. Next is the bedroom, but I do a quick stop at the front door to make sure it's locked and set the alarm. I take a few steps and peak up the stairs to make sure no one is standing at the top. Before I enter the bedroom, I turn around again to check that the front door is still locked. In the bedroom, I quickly pull open the door to check behind it. I lay on the floor to check under the bed. Open the closets, make sure they're clear. Then, in the bathroom, I look behind the door, in the cabinets and behind the shower door. *Someone could have been hiding and snuck in when you were in the bathroom.* I check the closets and under the bed again.

Once things feel okay in the bedroom I move upstairs. First the bathroom. Behind the door, curtain and in the cabinet. Next to the bedroom, behind or in any boxes or in the cabinet. Lastly, the other bedroom. Check behind boxes and in a closet. There's a mirror propped up against the wall that always gets my heart racing. My own reflection gets me, but I also fear that someone is going to appear behind me if I look in it for too long. I make my way back downstairs to the main level and do a quick look into the bedroom, hallway, and living room. I check all locks, alarms, and the basement door stop to make sure they're all how I left them. I tiptoe to the living room to turn on the TV, then go to the bedroom to change clothes.

Thought Log:

If I change clothes now and get as ready for bed as much as possible, then that's less moving I'll have to do in the bedroom after it gets dark.

Before opening the closet for my clothes, I check under the bed and clear the bathroom again.

Thought Log:

Someone could have been hiding and snuck in the bedroom when you were in the bathroom.

I check the closets and under the bed again. Once I'm changed, I check locks, alarms and door stop before opening the dining and living room curtains. If someone were to enter the house, my only hope is that someone outside will be able to see through the windows and help me somehow. I sit in the corner chair of the living room so I'm close to an exit. I watch TV but keep an eye on the living room doorway. Soon my stomach rumbles. I'm hungry, but unable to get up.

Thought Log:

If I move, then whoever is in the house will hear me and execute their plan to hurt me. Sitting quietly is the only thing that is safe.

After a while, the hunger gets bad, so bad that I start to become shaky. I tiptoe to the kitchen, but first make sure the locks, door stop, and alarms are all still set. I throw something in the microwave so I can get back to my "safe" chair as fast as possible. I think about using the bathroom while I'm up, but it's too risky. It can wait. My food is done, and I run back to my chair. I make it back safely this time without someone chasing me. I eat my food but keep my eye on the doorway and windows to make sure no one is looking in.

Forty minutes later, I must use the bathroom. I can't hold it any longer. I decide it's time to risk it, so I make a plan. Tiptoe to the hallway bathroom, check the locks and make it back as fast as you can. When you're going to the bathroom, leave the door open in order to keep an eye on the dining room so you will be able to see if anyone walks through. I execute my plan and make it to the bathroom safely.

Thought Log:

What if someone unlocked the door and turned off the alarms after I went into the bathroom?

I walk out and turn to verify the locks, alarm and doorstop are still as I left them. Now I need to get back to the chair where I'll stay until right before dark. The dark is the un-safest time. I must be in the bedroom with everything locked up before it gets dark.

Thought Log:

It's getting dark. No one has got me yet, but now is the time. Be ready to be assaulted, kidnapped and killed.

Close all the curtains. Check the locks, door stop and alarms. Turn the bedroom light on. Turn the rest of the house lights off. Go into the bedroom and lock the door. Check under the bed, closets and bathroom. Turn on the TV but check the guide to make sure nothing scary will be on during the night. Turn off the sleep timer so it stays on all night. Turn the air purifier on for extra noise. Pick a video to play on my phone for extra noise. Now that the noise is covered and the room is checked, time to decide on how much light is needed. "You're an adult, you don't need to keep the main light on all night" I tell myself.

Thought Log:

If I were to keep the main light on all night, then someone will see it and try to come inside to get me.

We have two desk lamps, so I turn the brighter one on.

Time to lay in bed. This is the time of night I hate the most because I know I will be attacked during the night when I'm most vulnerable. I always have a plan to get away by jumping out the bathroom window if needed, but I know someone will be waiting outside for me.

Thought Log:

If you don't lock the bathroom windows, then someone will come in to kill you. If you don't keep them unlocked though, you won't be able to escape.

Nothing I do will stop the attack, so I decide to leave the window unlocked. All I can do is try to delay the inevitable.

Before lying in bed, I check the bedroom lock and under the bed. I lay down on my back in the middle of the bed with my head propped up. If I can always see the bedroom and bathroom door, then I'll be able to get away faster. I pull the blankets all the way up to my neck with only my head out. I try to get comfortable, but it's difficult to do when I can't allow myself to move. I'm normally a side sleeper, but I can't do that on nights Cody is gone. I'm forced to sleep on my back and only turn my head in a way that I can get comfortable but still see both doors.

It's already been two hours since I got in bed, but I won't let myself fall asleep. I force myself to keep watching TV, because it's safer this way. A show comes on that makes no sense and I don't want to watch, but I can't change the channel because I already did my check to make sure no scary shows were on throughout the night. I force myself to keep watching the show when I hear a noise.

Thought Log:

Someone is in the house. They're going to come to the door, so I need to stare at the knob to wait for it to turn. Once they turn the knob, they're going to try to grab me as I run for the bathroom. They're going to tie me up to one of the dining room chairs. Another person will be outside as a backup that they'll call inside to help. I'll do my best to scream for help, but no one can hear me. I'm all alone. No one will find me until Cody gets home in a couple days.

My eyes don't leave the doorknob for an hour. Eventually my eyes start to get heavy as the anxiety lessens since there has not been another noise. Finally, I fall asleep but wake up only thirty minutes later. Time to check. Make sure the door is still locked, climb around the bed to look around the edges and peak into the bathroom. It all looks clear, so back under the covers in my usual position. Back to watching a bad TV show until I can fall asleep again. I continue this routine three more times until it's finally time to get up for work.

I check the door lock, under the bed, closets and the bathroom before locking myself in the bathroom to get ready. I keep the TV on, but also turn the music on to drown out any noise in the house. Throughout my shower, I open the shower door to check and make sure the bathroom door is still locked.

Thought Log:

It's a waiting game until someone makes it in and comes to grab me. Since I'm already undressed, it will be that much easier for them. How would I be able to escape if I'm not dressed? Would I just run down the street in hopes no one tries to assault me when I'm running for help? I need to get out so I can keep an eye on the bathroom lock.

I dry my hair with the blow dryer but angle myself so I can still see the lock. I avoid looking into the mirror. It's time to go back into the bedroom. I fully expect someone to be sitting on the bed, waiting to grab me. I tiptoe out of the bathroom and do my checks. Check the bedroom door lock, closets, and under the bed. Okay things are clear for now. Get dressed as fast as possible then get the heck out of the house. I hurry through the rest of my morning routine before booking it out of the house. I feel at ease as I pull my car out of the driveway. I'm safe. I survived the night alone.

During my drive, I think about the fact that this week, I must repeat this routine for three nights before Cody returns. Each day I will walk into work as if nothing happened. I'm used to this routine because I've lived it for years. On the outside I appear normal but, on the inside, the pain I have for my inability to be able to just do normal things, like sleep alone, continues to grow. I talk to Alex about my night, but never go into much detail.

"Cody was gone last night so that means I didn't get as much sleep as I normally do. I'm always too worried about someone coming inside the house."

"Well, he's coming back soon, right? At least you only must do it for a couple more nights."

All I hear is that my time on Earth is coming to an end. I survived last night but what about tonight?

Thought Log:

There's no way I'm going to make it through another night because whoever is coming after me is going to try tonight. Going back into my house just means that I'll be alone and unable to protect myself.

At 5pm, I pull into my garage and start my routine again. Check locks, alarms, door stop then check everywhere in the house besides the basement. Tiptoe around and only move when necessary. Get to bed before it gets dark. After an exhausting night of checking and paranoia, I crawl into bed and hear Cody's voice "babe, did you journal?" I know he would tell me to journal if he were here, so I should do it before trying to sleep for the night.

Journal Entry: Today I feel defeated. I feel kind of crazy and too messed up to get any better. I wish I had gotten help earlier so maybe my thoughts wouldn't be so severe and violent. I know I'm not crazy and I'll feel better in a couple days. I must be optimistic and recognize the OCD thoughts and talk myself down. It'll be better once Cody is home.

Chapter 3

Journal Entry: I feel so alone. No one understands how bad I am doing because I don't show that side of me. I just want to scream at how unfair this all is.

After grappling with this OCD diagnosis for a few weeks now, I know that I need to find people like me. For me to process how I feel about OCD, I need to find someone that has been through it already. I start to search online for support groups. I found a group specifically for people with OCD on Facebook. My head fills with reasons not to join the group.

Thought Log:

What if you talk about your obsessions and they're used against you? What if someone that you know is also in the group and tells everyone about your OCD? What if someone comes to find you to hurt you?

Research about the secrecy of Facebook groups and privacy settings is the only thing that somewhat eases the anxiety. Even then, it takes all my strength to push the request to join button.

Immediately after requesting to join, I regret it. I have no trust that my information is safe, and I know someone will be coming for me. A few minutes later, I'm accepted to join the group. Immediately I un-joined. I'm not ready to expose myself.

Instead of looking for other people to help me understand, I'll just figure it out myself. I download book after book about OCD to better understand what's wrong with me. The first book I choose to read is a memoir about a girl's endless routines she used as a child. Her mind was filled with constant worries that her thoughts caused someone to die and spread illnesses. I don't have those problems so obviously I'm fine. Plus, I don't even do any routines like she's describing. Even though my thoughts try to tell me that I'm fine, my anxiety starts to grow. The room is getting smaller with each word I read. I feel like I can't breathe but I also can't stop reading. I need to know how she got better.

In two hours, I've read half the book and am on the brink of a panic attack.

Thought Log:

Cody is going to leave you because of your OCD. He doesn't need to be with a person like you.

I jump out of bed and go to the kitchen. Cleaning always makes things better, plus that makes me a good wife. Cody won't leave if I clean enough.

I start by pulling the grates off the stove in order to wash them in the sink. Next, I wipe down the stove top and try my best to get every speck of food off. I'm starting to get hungry, but it can wait. I need to get this done first. While I wait for the stove grates to dry, I open the microwave that sits above the oven to clean it.

Thought Log:

If someone sees all the splattered food in here, they'll think I'm not good enough for Cody.

I scrub as hard as I can to get all the food cleaned up. My body starts to get sore from standing on my tip toes trying to reach. My legs are shaking but I can't stop. I look down and realize you can see finger smudges on the buttons for the stove. I must clean those or else it'll look like I've never cleaned this kitchen. I wipe them down as much as I can before noticing the same smudges on the microwave. I work tirelessly to make them appear spotless as if we never even use them.

Thought Log:

It's obvious to everyone that you never cook. You make Cody do it all because you can't cook anything and are a terrible wife. No one thinks you're good enough for him.

Next, I clean out the sink since there are water marks all over it. I spray it down with a cleaner, scrub it, rinse then dry it with a paper towel. I repeat the steps three times until all the water spots are gone and it looks acceptable. Now I was getting hungry. My legs are feeling weak and my whole body is getting shaky.

Thought Log:

A good wife would clean until things were done. You don't deserve food yet.

Okay now I need to do the counters. I spray cleaner and wipe down the counter, but instead of moving things, I just wipe around them. I'm getting tired and want to get done faster.

Thought Log:

Even if everything is clean, someone will see that spot and think you're a bad wife.

No, I don't need a break, I'll get it done right. I pull everything off the counters and clean again. Everything is being put back in their place when I notice some dust on top of the coffee can. I hate coffee, but Cody drinks it occasionally, so I might as well clean it off, so it looks better.

Thought Log:

What if he was doing some kind of contest with himself to see how dirty it can get? You just ruined everything. He's going to be so mad at you.

Dread consumes me as I contemplate what I've just done. There's no way to put the dust back, but maybe I can make it up to him. I'll dust the rest of the house. I really need to use the bathroom, but I can finish everything first. I don't need a break.

First, I'll dust the table, then all the shelves in the living room. I start to pull off the trinkets we have on the shelf and dust them all off. It makes me happy to look at everything we've collected since we moved here a few months ago.

Thought Log:

What if you put everything back and they look stupid, and everyone hates how it's arranged? Way to go, you ruined the house.

I snap back into cleaning mode and continue to dust. My whole body is covered in sweat because I'm so hungry and my body won't stop shaking. I quickly change into shorts and a tank top. Walking back into the living room after changing, I notice some cobwebs on the fireplace. I feel like I can't move as I stare at them.

Thought Log:

No one will think you're good enough once they see those cobwebs. You're disgusting.

Quick! Grab the vacuum and find all the cobwebs. I walk all through the house trying to find every cobweb I could see before anyone else notices them. Finally, I feel satisfied that I've gotten all of them, and I can finish up dusting. My stomach starts to hurt more from hunger pains and needing to use the bathroom, but I can't stop. Just a little more cleaning to do.

After completing the dusting in every room of the house, I start on the bathrooms. These are the biggest worries because to me, a gross bathroom is an indicator that I'm gross and not a good person. Plus, Cody deserves a clean bathroom. I scrub both bathrooms until it feels like there is nothing else to clean. Well now that the toilet is clean, I can't use it until Cody gets home and sees how clean it is. I want him to see that I cleaned everything. I can wait. It's fine.

Finally, I'm at the final step of my process, which is to vacuum the whole house. I know that I will be drenched in sweat by the time I finish vacuuming, but it's okay because at least the house will be clean. I start with the hallway, then the kitchen, dining room, bedroom and living room. Finally done! Thank goodness! It feels so good to finally be done so I can finally eat. I start to walk the vacuum back to the closet when I remember that I found a sticky spot on the kitchen floor when I was vacuuming.

Thought Log:

You're not a good wife if you don't clean that up.

I pull the mop out from the closet and start mopping the kitchen. In order to get the sticky spot, I get on my hands and knees trying my best to get it to come up. After ten minutes, the kitchen feels clean and presentable. Now I must clean the rest of the tile and hardwood with the mop. I make my way throughout the house to mop the bathrooms and bedroom. Returning the mop to the closet, I feel like I can barely walk anymore. I've waited too long to eat, but it's okay. The house is clean now so I'm a good wife and everyone will be able to see it if they come into the house. I grab some water and chips then sit on the couch to try to get rid of the shakiness. When I look at the clock, I realize I was cleaning for two hours. Cody is about to be home.

A few minutes later, I hear the back door open.

Thought Log:

When the back door opened, I knew it was likely Cody but also thought it'd be a stranger trying to break in to kidnap me.

I sit motionless waiting to see who would come around the corner into the living room.

"Hey babe," Cody says with a smile on his face. Thank goodness it's him. After giving me a kiss, he makes his way to the bathroom. "Did you clean? It smells good."

"Yeah, I did, I just got done actually." I'm relieved that he noticed and that he used the bathroom right away. Now, I can finally use the bathroom.

Cody starts to get situated in the living room while the anxiety from the book I read creeps back up. I feel bad putting this on him right when he gets home, but I know if I don't then I'm going to have a panic attack.

"So, I started to read about a girl's OCD from her childhood."

"How'd that go?"

"Well, it made me question if I even have OCD. I mean, I don't do anything like she does."

"I don't know babe. Maybe you should just wait and talk to Wanda about it during your next session."

I know he's right, but I need an answer now. If I do have OCD, then I need to get the answer as to how to make it better. My cousin, Max, is in school to be a psychiatrist, so I decide to reach out.

"Hey random question for you… have you ever worked with anyone that has OCD?"

He quickly responds "Hey! I don't have much experience with it, but I was trained in treatment for that a few years ago. I've never actually had a patient with an OCD diagnosis though."

My heart drops as the little hope I had in getting an answer was decreasing "Oh okay. Please don't tell anyone, but I was diagnosed with OCD recently. I'm in therapy for it but didn't know if you had some suggestions as I've been really struggling lately." Did I just admit to someone that I have OCD? Is he going to hate me now?

"I'll keep it to myself. I'm sorry you've been having a hard time with it. I can look for some more resources though! Is there anything specific you're looking for?"

Maybe it's going to be okay, "Right now I'm working on recognizing my irrational thoughts. I've been logging them and the amount that I'm having is a lot to handle. I used to be on medications when I was just diagnosed with anxiety, but decided to go off when they made me feel no emotions. Plus, all the thoughts were still there, just not the physical response."

"Well, it sounds like you're doing the right things. Looking at my training items, the gold standard treatment for OCD is exposure and response prevention so hopefully your therapist starts doing that with you. A lot of the time, things can appear to get a lot worse for a short time before they start to get better while in treatment. It sucks, but it happens to a lot of people. If you want, I can email you some things I have about OCD treatment? The information would at least be reliable and may give some insight on how treatment goes."

"Yeah, that'd be great! I'm all about doing research so I'll accept anything I can get. Thanks so much!" Shortly after our conversation, Max emailed me a huge chapter from one of the books he has in his office. Looking through the readings just gives me the same anxiety I felt when I read the memoir earlier in the day. It's so much information that I can't comprehend how I'll ever get better if I can't even understand it. I realize that it's time to face the facts. I'm not going to be able to handle this on my own. It's time to revisit the idea of finding other people with OCD. I search Facebook again for other groups for people with OCD. I don't want to re-join the group I joined and unjoined earlier because I don't want them to judge me for chickening out. After about thirty minutes, I finally find one that I decide to try. Moments later, the leaders of the group accept me so I can see all the posts from other members. The first couple of posts are about people being hospitalized for their OCD. I can't do this. I need time. I want to focus on something other than OCD for a little bit. I exit out of the app and start to watch the show Cody has on.

Journal Entry: I still kind of wish I had never found out. It feels like things will never go back to normal. I just want this initial chapter of OCD to be over. Let's move on already. Hopefully I can keep being open with Wanda and she can help me move forward.

After reflecting for a few days to let my anxiety decrease, I decided to take the plunge and open the Facebook group again. I start looking through the posts and for once, I feel less alone. Maybe it is safe to write a post.

Thought Log:

Don't do it. Someone will come break into your house if you ever admit what you do to keep yourself safe.

I wrestle back and forth about whether it's safe or not to start talking about my OCD. Finally, after typing and retyping a post for half an hour, I decide it was worth the risk.

"New to this group and new to my OCD diagnosis. My intrusive thoughts involve being worried I will be hurt. It generally doesn't matter where I am, but thoughts will come up about fears someone will try to assault me, kidnap me, etc. Anyone else have these types of thoughts?"

Thought Log:

No one cares about your stupid OCD. Everyone there is handling it fine. You're the one that is letting it take over.

After refreshing my phone for an hour, a notification pops up. Someone commented on my post in the group.

"I'm in the same boat. It's hard, but you'll get through it. Thinking of you!" I can't help but smile. Someone finally said they understood! Someone else is in fact going through this. I'm not completely alone!

Throughout the night, people continue to comment and give nothing but their support. It feels so empowering to admit what I have been struggling with. More than just Cody, Alex and Max now know what I am going through. My true self doesn't feel so hidden anymore.

Journal Entry: I feel so good and understood. I got to share more about myself than usual and I hope I keep using the group to help me. Now I just need to work on myself and continue to improve.

Now that I can finally admit that I have OCD, time to figure out if there is somewhere I can talk about it in person. I keep up with the Facebook page daily and post when I need, but I want something more. I search for what feels like hours until I finally find something.

"Mental Illness Support Group for adults who have symptoms of a mental health condition."

Although it's not specific to OCD, maybe this is worth checking out? There's a group later in the day that I can join.

Thought Log:

Worried that if I brought a stress ball to the support group, someone would ask to see it, then put a microchip in it, or poison it.

I walk into the building with my guard up. So far all I see is an empty lobby with a few closed doors that appear to be offices. No one is here that I can see. After standing in the lobby doorway for a minute trying to figure out where to go, I hear someone moving so I turn to my left and peek into a room to see someone sitting there. She has red hair and is wearing a purple sweater with a pair of jeans.

"Hi, I'm Amy, one of the facilitators for the support group! What's your name?"

"Hi, I'm Andrea." I look around to see a big table with empty chairs set up around it. I'm the first one here.

"Go ahead and take a seat where you want, and we'll wait for people to get here." I nod as I make my way to the corner seat, as far away from Amy as I can. I pull out my phone to avoid any conversation.

"Hey Andrea, do you want some water or a snack?"

"No thank you."

"Okay, well they're right there, so grab them whenever. Also, the bathroom is right through that hallway. Plus, there are a ton of resources out in the lobby if you ever want to look through them. They're free to grab at any time."

"Okay, thank you." Thankfully right then someone else walks in that Amy already knows so I can keep my head down until group starts. After ten minutes of staring blankly at my phone, I look up to see Amy shut the door. We are ready to start. I look around and there is a second facilitator sitting next to Amy now. Two seats away there is a man with black hair and a blue shirt on. He is very smiley and appears to come to groups often with how much he's talking with the facilitators. On the other side of me sits a woman with brown hair who looks just as shy as me. She has a notebook in front of her that she keeps fidgeting with.

"So first we're going to go around and summarize what's been going on in our lives recently. If you don't feel comfortable, then feel free to pass. Andrea, since you're new here, I just want to make sure you know that you can share as much or as little as you'd like. Some people come in and just listen while others like to talk about their lives." I snap back into it.

Thought Log:

Don't share. If you share your paranoia, someone is going to follow you to your car and hurt you.

I try to focus as Amy starts to share how she's been doing recently. "So, I've been doing okay. I'm still working in therapy and looking for some new volunteer work. It's been stressful and I've been struggling to handle my anxiety. It's a lot to deal with so I know I must use my coping skills like writing and spending time with my friends." Wow, I feel the same way.

Next the man in the blue shirt starts to share. "I've been doing well actually. The last time I was here I wasn't doing too well, but I got my meds changed which has been helping me a lot. I even pushed myself to try something new at the apartment complex I live in. They have these get-togethers and usually I don't go because my anxiety is too high, but not this time. I was feeling good, so I joined and met some new people." Amy and the other facilitator praise him for pushing himself and going out of his comfort zone.

Now it's my turn. Time to decide what to do.

Thought Log:

If you don't share, you're pathetic and weak because you're not brave enough to talk about it. But if you do share, then you're going to be killed because someone is going to play into your compulsions.

"Well, I'm here because I was recently diagnosed with OCD, and I've just been struggling a lot." I put my head down to avoid eye contact, "I'm realizing that I've had it for basically my entire life, but no one figured it out until now." I raise my head slightly to see everyone's reactions. "I'm twenty-four years old and someone just now figured out how sick I am. My mind is constantly filled with terrible thoughts about how I'm going to be hurt. I walk down the sidewalk and immediately assume whoever is walking towards me is about to assault, kidnap then kill me. I have no hope that I'll ever get better because over the years the fear has just gotten worse, so what's the point in trying?" Silence took over as everyone looks at me, waiting to make sure I'm done. I grab the stress ball I brought with me. I stare at my lap and squeeze it until my hand is sore, trying to find relief from the anger and sadness I'm feeling.

The facilitator sitting next to Amy speaks up first, "It sounds like you've had a lot happening lately. I think all of us here have been through the same feelings when we were first diagnosed." I look around the room to see everyone nodding their heads.

My confidence starts to grow as I continue, "It's just so hard because I'm realizing that not many people really know about OCD. All I hear is "oh I'm so OCD" when they just mean that they're organized. They have no clue how miserable it is. If I had a choice not to do the things I do, then I would gladly just not do them. People don't realize that every compulsion I have has a reason behind it. It's not something I can just stop doing."

This time Amy speaks up, "You have a right to be angry. I've heard the same things about OCD."

The shy girl speaks for the first time, "I didn't have anyone understand when I was diagnosed with Bipolar disorder. It was hard to try to educate people on what it is."

"Yep, same for me," I look over to see the man in the blue shirt making direct eye contact. "It can be hard. What types of things have you been doing to try to cope with it?"

Am I even trying to cope? I feel like I've just been in the being angry phase and sad phase. "Well, I've been just trying to do research to understand what OCD is, but it's just been making me more anxious. I will see my therapist tomorrow so hopefully that helps a little. Otherwise, I journal every night but that's about my only coping skill right now."

Throughout the rest of the group, I feel pure gratitude that I had the confidence to attend the group and speak up. I've finally found a place to be myself and express all the emotions I've been feeling, good and bad.

Journal Entry: Today was better but I still want to know how to get rid of the thoughts. I need help and it's scary not knowing how to help yourself. I want to know more, so I can understand myself better. I'm simply confused and feel like I just misunderstand myself. I need help and that's okay.

The next day I get ready for another session with Wanda. I want to find the underlying cause of all the questions I have.

After we make it through all my logs, Wanda asks, "What's it been like to write down all your irrational thoughts?"

"Well, I can't believe I have so many bad thoughts. I didn't even realize they were so bad and violent. No wonder why I'm always so paranoid."

"How many of them were you able to recognize as irrational?"

I feel embarrassed by my answer, so I pick up a fidget cube Wanda has on the table between us. "Most of the time I just argued with myself if it was irrational or not. I'd initially think it was irrational but then talk myself out of it. Honestly, it felt like I had no clue what was real vs. not real. The only one that I knew was irrational was the fear I had before I went to the support group for the first time. I knew no one would do something to the stress ball I brought, but I still fought myself if I should bring it or not. Eventually I decided to bring it, but I was still reserved about it. I didn't want anyone else to touch it."

"How was it going to the support group?"

"It was helpful! I felt welcome and that I could talk about anything to them. They all have had similar experiences when they were first diagnosed, which helped."

"Good, I'm happy that you went looking for support and then actually went. Do you think you'll keep going?"

"Yeah, I hope so," then I think back to all my research in the past week and the anxiety it gave me. "Oh, also I did try to learn more about OCD, and it didn't end great. I read about half of a memoir and almost went into a panic attack. Then I reached out to my cousin who's studying to be a psychiatrist and he sent me some more information about it. None of the information helped much because it made me more confused. I know that I have OCD, but none of what I read about matched with what was in the books."

"Woah, you need to slow down on reading and researching things. Treatment takes time and you don't need to 'ace' therapy. It'll take as long as it'll take."

Wanda is right. I must do this the right way. Leaving the session, I feel like I have more hope than I have ever had since I was diagnosed.

Chapter 4

Journal Entry: Okay, I can do this. This is going to take time and I won't just get better without going through some heartache. Things are looking up though because I'm finally starting to learn how to recognize these thoughts. Go me!

A few days after my last session with Wanda, I'm driving to work dreading the long day ahead of me. The first thing I have for the day is to go to the courthouse for a meeting, then to a couple houses to see clients. Unfortunately, I scheduled my appointments too close together, so I'm worried about making it to everything and being on time. I'm trying to review how I can make it all work without disappointing anyone.

I pull in my work parking lot and immediately start to make my way to the courthouse on foot. The building is several blocks away and I never feel safe walking around, so my head stays on a swivel.

Thought Log:

Saw a guy walking towards me, thought he was going to whip around and touch me.

There was a tarp laying on the ground, I thought it was a dead body.

I entered the courthouse and made a scenario to see if there was a shooter and how I would get free.

After sitting through my meeting, I look at my watch and realize it is 10:25am. I need to make it back to my car quickly to get to my next client's house by 10:45am. I'm breathing heavily and starting to feel nauseous from the fast walking, but also from worrying that I'll be late.

Thought Log:

Thought about if during my home visit, someone would stab me in the chest. Visualized it and thought about it the whole way to the house and during my visit. Hard to get out of my mind.

Walking out of that house feels like a relief. I wasn't hurt and now I must go back to my office to take a short break before my next home visit. Driving back, I start to review the first meeting I had this morning. It was a meeting for the workers of a common client and one of the other workers discussed their lack of hope they feel for the family. Sometimes I feel the same way about them, but I like to be an optimistic social worker. The things I said during the meeting start to repeat in my head, "They try hard to be there for each other, but sometimes they get caught up in their own things so it's hard to take views from people outside their family. The family is protective of each other, which is a strength." Did I sound dumb when saying that? What if it's not true and I'm just a bad worker? Did all the other workers in the room roll their eyes at me? Even though I'm driving, I start to pretend to type with my toes again "the family is protective. The family is protective. The family is protective." I pull in my assigned parking spot and continue to nitpick the whole conversation. Am I even helping the family at all? What if they're not protective and they're just hiding something? Walking into my office, I'm happy to see Alex sitting at her desk so I can pull myself out of the loop. "Morning, how's it going?"

"Oh good. Have you been out doing visits already?"

"Yeah, I just got back from a house visit and right away this morning I had to go down to the courthouse. This is the first time I get to just sit down for a minute." It feels so nice to sit in my chair and let my legs rest, but I can't rest for too long. I have work to do and there is another concern on my mind. "So, Alex, I know this may sound crazy, but one of my other client's hasn't been responding to me for a while. For some reason I have this weird feeling that they did something to their kids."

"Why do you think that?"

"I really have no reason to think it. It's just because they haven't answered which they usually do."

"Irrational thought?" Alex caught me.

"Crap, yeah probably." I'm going to add it to my log, which feels like defeat. I hate adding to my log. It makes me feel more mentally ill each time.

Not even thirty minutes after my conversation with Alex about my paranoid thought, I receive confirmation that everything is okay with my client.

"Well Alex, you were right. I was paranoid for no reason."

"Glad I could help. Do you feel okay now?"

"Yeah, I mean I'm glad that no one is hurt and that I heard back." I am too worried about the rest of my day to continue worrying about my other clients. I am still trying to figure out how to make the rest of my meetings work. Google maps tells me the best way to go in the shortest amount of time. I put them into my phone so all I must do is push a button so I will be ready. My paperwork is neatly piled on my desk so I can grab it and go. My leg won't stop bouncing in anticipation of when I can leave. I don't want to get to my client's house too early, but I don't want to be late either. 12:47pm will be the time I can leave my office to get there at the perfect time. I stare at the clock waiting. 12:45… 12:46… come on already! 12:47 finally I can go!

I fast walk to the parking lot to get in my car to see that a fire truck is blocking the exit. Anxiety sets in as I panic about being late. How am I supposed to stay on my schedule if I can't leave? Should I just cancel or try to make it still? I'll be late to my appointment after this one if I don't leave right now.

Thought Log:

Don't cancel. You'd be a terrible caseworker if you cancelled because you didn't find a way to get there. Something bad will happen if you don't just figure it out.

I reach out to my client, Doug, to let him know that I may be late. He's understanding as usual and said it's fine to get there whenever I can. I make my way back to my desk to tell Alex what's going on. I laugh and make jokes about how random the firetruck is, but inside I feel like I'm being squeezed by a boa constrictor. My plan is ruined and there's nothing I can do. If I try to leave, then I'll hit another car. What if I get a ticket for interfering with whatever the firefighters are trying to do? I can get someone else to drive me and just drop me off, but then I'd be stuck at Doug's house with no car, which is too dangerous. I walk back and forth between my desk and the parking lot three times to check if it's gone. Each time it's still there, I create a new plan in my head as to how I can make the rest of the day work.

Twenty minutes later, the truck finally moves. I rush to Doug's home. Pulling up, I maneuver my car to park on the street, so I won't get blocked in. Also, I want to keep my eyes out for his dog. She sits in the front yard on a leash with the goal of protecting the house and her family. We lock eyes as she makes it clear I'm not welcome on her property. I feel paralyzed in fear and no confidence in my ability to protect myself if she gets too close. Seeing me outside, Doug comes out knowing that his dog is protective and doesn't like strangers. He holds her back as I enter the house to do a check-in.

"Well Doug, how are things going since we last talked?"

"They're okay. I just have a lot going on right now." The dog starts to bark as she hears Doug's voice. I try my best to stay focused on Doug as my head fills with worry. What if the dog can get through the door? There are other dogs in this area, what if they all gang up and come through the door together?

"Would it help if we made a list, and I can take over some tasks to help out?" For the next thirty minutes, Doug and I worked together to determine how to problem solve and decrease his anxiety. Throughout the visit, the barking decreases, as well as my anxiety. My confidence has grown in my ability to help Doug and show him as much support as I can.

"Why don't you go out the back door so you can pass the dog without her bothering you," Doug says as he leads me through the house. I walk out the door and say my goodbyes, but my mind has already moved on. *How am I going to make it to my next meeting without being late?* Suddenly, I feel pressure on my right thigh. I quickly realize the dog is attacking me. All that goes through my head is that the dog is loose and there is no getting away. I have no hope of survival. I try to run to my left, but I feel the teeth puncture through my left thigh. My body goes into flight mode. I continue to try running to my left away from the house. Finally, the dog is off, and I realize I'm in the middle of the road. I look around the street as my shoes and the paperwork I was holding is thrown across the yard. Doug comes running towards me, "Oh my gosh, did she get you?"

I look down at my thighs, my pants are ripped with blood starting to seep through. *My anger grows as I think of course she freaking did! Look at my pants!* Instead, I hold back the tears as I try to talk. "Yeah, I think she did," as I point to the holes in my pants. "Let's just touch base later today and figure out when we can meet next," I say while starting the walk to my car. I keep my head down to hide the tears that are starting to roll down my cheeks. I look to my left to see a neighbor staring. I want to scream, "Why didn't you help me? Why did NO ONE help?"

Sitting in my car still outside Doug's house, I look at the notebook I dropped during the attack. There is a bite mark that went all the way through. Looking down, I become more concerned about what my legs look like underneath my pants. I contemplate what to do next. Maybe I can still make it to my next session and then worry about my legs later. I quickly learn it's not an option as the number of tears increases. I know I won't be able to remain professional in my next session. Maybe if I explain what happened, then they won't blame me for having to cancel. Before driving off, I send a text to my client, "Hey just so you know, I need to cancel our meeting. I was bitten by a client's dog and will likely need to go to the doctor. I'll reach out tomorrow to reschedule. Sorry!"

Now I need to talk to Cody. He answers the phone after the first ring but all I can hear is him singing. He pocket answered. The knot in my throat is growing as I try to call for him "Cody? Cody?" but it only comes out in a whisper. Suddenly I start screaming "CODY! CODY! CODY, PLEASE ANSWER ME!" as all the emotions I have been holding back start to come out. I scream until my throat hurts and my face is covered in tears. He still can't hear me. By the time I realize that I was driving, I'm already pulling into my office parking lot. I send Cody a text before walking inside. I start to type out "I was attacked by a dog, and I don't know what to do" but I downgrade it to "I was bit by a dog, and I don't know what to do." *I'm being dramatic and pathetic for screaming into the phone like that. It's just a bite. I need to grow up.*

I do my best to hide my face when I enter the building so no one can tell I had been crying. My head is telling me *you're weak and pathetic. If anyone else had been bitten, they would be fine and would have gone to that next meeting. That client needed you and you failed by not being there for them.*

The only place I think to go is my office. Alex is the only one there. I slam my notebook on my desk before saying, "A freaking dog bit me," in a way to sound more angry than terrified. I want to appear strong.

"If you go to the bathroom downstairs, you should have more room to be able to see your legs," Alex responds. I make my way to the bathroom so I can finally see the damage. Pulling my pants down, the pain starts to grow. Immediately I see the skin is broken on both legs. Panic sets in as I think of rabies and all the other diseases that I am now susceptible to. I just want to get out of here and get back to my car to call Cody.

Eventually I get permission to use workman's compensation and head to urgent care. As soon as I get back into my car, I try to call Cody with no luck. Next, I try to call my mom, again with no luck. I scream, "Why is no one answering me?" *Who else can I call?* I put my phone down because the road is getting blurry from all the tears. Right then my mom calls back and immediately knows something is wrong. I manage to get out, "a dog bit me, and it's bad."

"You need to pull over," she tells me.

"I can't! There's nowhere that's safe to do that. I just need to get to the doctor!" I try to tell her, in more detail, what happened, but it comes out in one big ramble. "I was at a family's house and the dog was out front on a leash. The owner told me she wasn't nice, so she kept us separated. So, when I went to leave the house, I went out a different door to avoid the dog. Then suddenly it was on my leg. I don't know what happened! Both my legs are bit!" I look down and see more blood seeping from my pants. "Oh my gosh, the blood is starting to come through my pants more."

"Do you have anything to wipe it off with?" I can hear my mom's voice starting to get shaky.

"No, I don't have anything in here." At this point, my tears are starting to dry, and I feel like I'm starting to be overdramatic again. It is the perfect opportunity to turn this situation around. So, I start to laugh "Man these are my favorite pants too! Now I have to get some new ones."

First, she laughs along, "I'll buy you new pants Andrea!" but then her voice becomes concerned again. "Do you want me to come meet you at the doctor's office?"

Don't disrupt her day. She has other things she can do. "No, it's fine. Plus, by the time you get there, I'll be done anyways." Deep down it feels like my heart is breaking because all I want is someone to be there with me. I don't want to be strong anymore.

I want someone to manage everything so I can cry. I don't even want to be driving myself right now. Why did I tell her no?

The bleeding continues to get stronger as I walk into urgent care. I tell the nurses at check-in, so they give me a Kleenex box to stop the bleeding while they check me in. Thankfully, they realize soon enough they don't want blood all over their waiting room and take me back into one of the patient rooms. The nurse gives me a robe and tells me to pull my pants down so the doctor can see the bites. Once she leaves and I do as she asks, I get a full view of my legs. I take some quick pictures before the doctor comes in. He looks at the marks with little to no reaction. *Am I overreacting?* He thinks it's not that big of a deal so maybe I shouldn't have been crying.

"We can't stitch you up because they can get infected that way. So, we just need to clean them out then put bandages over them." When he's done, I look down to see two giant patches on my legs. "Now we need to call animal control so you can talk to them. You can't leave until they get here and sometimes it can take a while." The doctor leaves me alone to stare at my jeans ripped and stained with blood. My phone starts to go crazy with messages from my mom, dad, sister, and Cody. All of them ask if I need them, but my pride won't let me accept the help. I tell them all that I'm okay. I send the pictures of the bites that I took before the doctor patched them up. They respond with shock. *So, is it okay that I cried?*

Surprisingly, it only takes around twenty minutes for animal control to walk into the room. I'm already dressed. Both workers gasp when they see the pictures. *Okay, so it is important.* Even though they are in shock, I still don't want anyone's pity, because if I don't act strong, then that means I'm not strong. Plus, other people have indicated it's not a big deal, so why blow it out of proportion? *You're fine. Everything is fine.*

I decide I need to go back to my office. I pull up, I look down and realize my pants are still covered in blood and have very visible holes in them. My legs are already swelling and in addition to the bandages, my thighs look five times bigger than they are. My face is covered in dried tears and my clothes feel gross from how much I have been sweating. I look in my car mirror and notice how terrible I look.

Thought Log:

Made scenario about being ridiculed about how I look and being written up.

Do I go in and risk someone seeing me like this, or do I just go home? Finally, I decide it's worth going inside to finish the workday. Appearing strong is more important than how my body and clothes look. Although, all I really want is a nap.

I go to my desk but only Alex is still working. She looks at me surprised, "Um what are you doing here? I figured you'd just go home?" I can feel her eyes looking at my thighs.

I quickly sit, so she can't see how bad I really look. "No, I'm fine, I figured I would come back and finish up the incident report and whatever else I need to do." Alex looks at me concerned but I reassure her. "I talked with animal control and they're going to go check out the dog. They're going to make sure I don't need rabies shots or anything, but I should be fine. All I need is to wear bandages for a few days until they stop bleeding."

I turn on my computer to read my emails and stop at one I have from one of the managers, Marcy.

Marcy: Andrea, I'm sorry to hear about what happened. How awful. Please let me know if you need anything at all.

I reply: Hey thanks for reaching out. I got my legs patched up with bandages and doing okay right now. I'm back in the office so I can fill out the incident report.

I start to talk to Alex to distract from the pain that is running through my legs, "Oh my gosh I'm so tired."

Alex laughs, "I mean probably, you did get attacked today."

"No, that probably has nothing to do with it," I respond sarcastically. I lay my head on my desk to close my eyes for a minute. It's the first time I've slowed down enough to start comprehending the attack. I realize that I don't remember seeing the dog at all. *Did I black out? How do I not remember seeing the dog before, during or after it happened?* Right then, my computer chimes with an incoming email.

Marcy: Wow you're a trooper for coming back to the office today. Would you be okay if I let other staff know about what happened? I'm sure they would like to express their concerns and their gratitude that you're safe.

I replied: Yeah, that's fine.

My coworkers knowing will be a good thing. I can prove how strong I am.

I start the incident report. The easy part is the location, time, etc., but now it's time to write what happened. My mind goes blank. Was I in Doug's yard when the dog attacked me? Was it my fault or was I on the road and the dog's chain was just too long that it could still reach me?

I need input from Alex. "So, I'm filling out this incident report and I'm realizing I don't really remember anything. I'm like 99% sure I was on the road, but I don't know."

"If you think you were on the road, then I'm sure you were. Especially since you were aware of the dog when you got there." Alex's response reassures me to trust myself and I know that I did not put myself in harm's way on purpose.

I finish the incident report and decide I'm too tired to continue working. Plus, I really want to get out of these clothes.

Thought Log:

You smell and everyone is going to talk about how terrible you look. No one cares about your legs.

Driving home feels like one big blur. I pull into the garage not remembering any of the drive.

Thought Log:

You could've killed someone because you're too wrapped up in your legs.

Exhaustion takes over as soon as I sit down on the couch. The puncture wounds from the dog's teeth start to pulse in pain. *I can't take it anymore!* I need to change into something that won't press on the wounds. It's time to face my legs.

I can barely look down after I remove the bandages to let the wounds get some air. The left one doesn't look as bad, just a small puncture wound, then a long cut next to the tooth mark. On the top are some scrapes in the shape of the dog's top jaw. My right leg is harder to look at. There are two puncture wounds closer together that look so deep and are continuously filling with blood. I open the pictures I took from the doctor's office and can't help but stare at them.

Thought Log:

Your legs are disgusting. Plus, everyone saw you crying like a child and looking like a weak person that can't even manage a couple dog bites. It wasn't even a big deal, but you made it a big deal. You cried into the phone and screamed Cody's name like a pathetic person.

Before I head back to the couch, I feel like journaling, so I don't have to do it tonight.

Journal Entry: Well today sucked. I can't believe that happened. I should've just canceled my session after my car was blocked, but I knew Doug needed me. It's not a big deal though. I'll get through it fine. It's fine.

Finally, I decide it's time to cover my legs with a blanket because it's easier to hide them than admit what was bound to happen. My life and my body are about to change. Not only will my legs be scarred for life, but so will the rest of me.

Chapter 5

Returning to work the day after the dog attack feels like I have a stamp on my forehead saying, "look at me, I was hurt yesterday." I feel this weird energy around me that makes me scared to leave my desk. My legs feel glued to my chair. I need to check my mailbox, but I can't get myself to move. At my desk, I'm safe.

It takes a while, but eventually I gain the confidence to start walking around. All the movement causes blood to start soaking through my bandages and spots start to appear through my jeans. My legs are stiff and it's obvious I'm walking differently. One of my coworkers points out the spot on my pants. I try to cover it with my hand but there's no hiding what happened.

Thought Log:

Your legs are gross, and no one wants to see them. Your body is ruined.

Everywhere I go, people notice me, whether I like it or not. The comments and questions start, but I have no answers. "Why did you let it bite both your legs?" asks a coworker who appears shocked by the pictures of the bites.

"I don't know," I try to put a smile on my face while holding back tears, "I don't really remember what happened. I only remember feeling one of the punctures on my left leg."

I try to hide at my desk, but there's almost a continuous cycle of people coming in to check on me. "Next time you should punch it in the face." Really? How about we set a dog after you and we can see if that's your first response. "That dog should be put down immediately." I don't blame the dog. I blame the owner. "Rrrrruff! Rrrrruff! Sorry, that was mean, but I just had to!" Well, that's just rude. "It's a good thing you didn't fall down or else you would've been really hurt." Are you saying that I'm not hurt now? "You've been through something so traumatic." Is it traumatic? I'm still doing my best to be strong. "Don't say anything negative about the breed of dog that attacked you." I wasn't. You asked what type of dog attacked me, I told you, then you became defensive. Again, I don't blame the dog or the breed.

I sit at my desk exhausted from everyone approaching me. I feel like an outsider. I don't feel welcome anymore. Instead of feeling strong, I feel weaker and weaker with each comment someone makes until one of my closest co-workers comes to my desk with the saddest eyes. She looks at me with so much care and worry, "someone told me you were hurt yesterday, and I was hoping you weren't going to be here. Why aren't you at home?" she asks.

"I'm fine. I can still walk." I pull out the pictures of my legs to show her the bite marks. She gasps and looks like she's about to cry. She's always been protective of me. When I broke my toe on the job a few months prior, she told me to get in her car to drive me to urgent care. That's what I want now. I want someone to take control because I don't know how to handle it. Am I supposed to be crying, angry, laughing, or all the above? Instead, all I feel is grief. I'm grieving how life was finally starting to feel good before the attack. I'm grieving the loss of any safety I felt before that is now gone. I'm grieving that my legs will never look the same. I want to scream at every person that comes to ask me about the attack, but also break down and cry. I want to talk about everything that happened, but also not speak for the next week. I want to continue my normal routine to provide some normalcy, but also curl up in the fetal position in bed. I don't do any of what I want though. Instead, I put a smile on my face and do what I always do. Focus on helping other people with their own problems and avoid mine.

I have a meeting scheduled at a school that I need to go to. Alex tries to convince me to stay in the office, but I won't listen. "No, it's fine. I told this girl that I'd come see her today and I can't let her down." Walking to my car, I can feel the blood from the bites start to pool and spill into the bandage. I look down and hope that no other spots will start to appear. *Please, just let me get through the day.*

Journal Entry: What's wrong with me? I just feel an overwhelming sadness taking over at the weirdest times.

It's finally the weekend. I have three days off and it couldn't come at a better time. My legs are starting to become more bruised each day. I can't help but look at pictures of my thighs from before the attack. It took me years to feel comfortable wearing shorts because I was so self-conscious of my thighs. Now that I'm confident, my thighs are bloody and bruised. Is this a sign that I should be embarrassed by my body? Maybe I shouldn't have been wearing shorts this whole time. Cody and I were invited to a party that will be outside, but it's ninety degrees. I go back and forth between what to wear throughout the whole morning.

Thought Log:

If you wear shorts, everyone will see your gross legs and ask too many questions. If you don't wear shorts, then you're the worst kind of woman. You're letting vanity take over and not being your true self.

"Cody what should I do? The bites won't stop bleeding, so I still need to wear the bandages. So, if I wear shorts, they'll be so obvious. If I wear jeans, then I'm backtracking on all the progress I took years to make!" It feels like such a small problem to worry about, but it also feels like the biggest step. It's my way of deciding if I'm going to embrace the change in my legs, or if I am going to hide.

"Do whatever you want. You're probably going to get hot in jeans, so just wear shorts." Cody reassures me. He was the first one to convince me to start wearing shorts that don't go all the way to my knee. Soon after we started dating, my self-esteem grew higher than it had ever been. Because of Cody, I am finally comfortable with my body. He has helped me learn my potential and gain confidence.

"Okay screw it. I'm going to wear shorts!" I'm proud of myself, "I worked for years to wear shorts and I'm not going to let this ruin that for me. I can't backtrack."

At the outing, people stare and ask questions, as expected. The event ended up being inside because of the heat so I didn't need to wear shorts. My confidence slowly drifts away the more we sit in the air conditioning.

Thought Log:

You're just wearing shorts for attention. Everyone is making fun of you for being so obvious about it.

I do my best to push the negative thoughts out of my head, but I can see people trying to evaluate me. They're trying to see how I'm doing. Then a dog approaches me. I feel ten eyes dart over to me to see how I react. Don't appear weak. Don't let anyone see you break. I pet the dog with no problem. My mom appears shocked, "Wow, I wasn't sure how you'd react to dogs now."

"Well, I've met that dog before, so I feel okay." I had met the dog before and I told myself that I'm okay, but deep down I'm screaming. I imagine a miniature version of myself, trapped in my brain screaming to get out "HELP ME!" I imagine that I'm pounding on the inside of my head "Please I need help! I'm not okay but I can't say that." When I realize no one is coming, I imagine falling to the floor with my legs pulled to my chest. In a whisper, I say "Please someone notice how broken I am." But no one can hear me.

Journal Entry: You're more than your bites. You know they're there and they will be there your entire life. It's part of your story now.

It's Monday night and my three-day weekend is almost over. My legs have finally stopped bleeding. I don't need to wear the bandages anymore, but the whole front of my thighs are covered in bruises. I do my best to avoid looking at them, but I can't get away. Anytime I go to the bathroom, I'm forced to see them. Anytime I need to change my pants, I'm forced to see them. I can see and feel how much worse the bites are looking. Pain is constantly running through the bites. The puncture wounds are starting to scab causing my thighs to itch like crazy.

Before bed, I look at my calendar for tomorrow. I'm scheduled to see a client with another dog. My throat feels like it's about to close and my hands shake while I'm trying to hold my phone. "Cody, I'm supposed go to a client's house tomorrow that has a dog that the owner says is mean. They usually lock it up before they open the door, but what if they don't this time?" I don't let on how much terror I feel.

"They've done it every time before, right? I'm sure they'll do it this time. To be safe, just remind the family that they need to make sure to lock it up before you get there."

I barely sleep through the night. All I can think about is coming face to face with this dog. All I think about is if it attacks me, this time I won't be so lucky. This time I will fall, and it'll attack my face. There is no chance I'll make it out alive from a second dog attack.

Thought Log:

Tomorrow is your last day alive. That dog is going to rip you apart.

The dog is going to jump up on you and no one will hear your screams. You'll be all alone.

If you tell your client that she needs to lock up the dog, then she's going to yell at you and let it go loose so it can attack you. She'll teach it a command to know when it was time to attack.

The dog is going to burst through the house window and try to get you while you're inside your car.

You're going to lose your job if you don't just suck it up and go to the houses with dogs. No one will care that you're scared. Get over it.

I need to put running shoes on or else I won't be able to run away from the dog when it attacks me.

Don't wear the same shirt as you wore when you were attacked the first time. If you wear the same shirt, then the dog is going to know and will certainly attack you.

Going into work, I drive as slow as I can. I do my best to stay calm by taking deep breaths and using one of my fidget toys that I keep in my car. In the meantime, all I can do is repeat the phrase, "Dogs are dangerous. Dogs are dangerous. Dogs are dangerous."

I do what I can to distract myself at work, but nothing is working. All that's on my mind is having to see the dog at 11am. I can't tear my eyes off my clock. It's 10am.

Thought Log:

Only an hour left until another part of your body is ruined by a dog. This time don't cry.

Finally, I work up the courage to send a text to my client, "Hey, hope things are going well! Just a reminder, when I come to pick you up today, please remember to lock the dog up before opening the door. Thanks, see you soon!"

I anxiously wait for the reply that will tell me that I'm pathetic for being scared. Instead, she replies, "Yep of course." Okay, nothing to worry about. It will all be okay.

I pull in the driveway and as usual, the dog stares at me through the window. Just as the other dog, this one doesn't like people on his property either. I get out of the car and start walking up to the door. The dog's barking grows louder and louder. *Dogs are dangerous. Dogs are dangerous. Dogs are dangerous*, runs through my head. I knock on the door then take a few steps back to create as much distance as possible. I'm waiting for the door to open for what feels like hours. I want to appear normal by looking around and at my phone, but it's all a ruse. My brain is telling me to run. My legs feel weak. My shoulders have been tensed up so much that they're sore. My hands are clammy along with the rest of my body. I want nothing more than to be back in my car where I feel safe.

The door opens and I smile when I see Rose start to come out. Suddenly, the dog is trying to get out of the door with all its might. I freeze as I hear it growling at me, ready to attack. Rose drops down to block the dog with her body and she closes the door. My heart is pounding. Every fear I had throughout the night felt like it just came true. Even though the dog never got to me, I still feel attacked in a way. I wait in dread for the door to open, fearful the dog will be there again. I think about waiting in my car, but that would make me a wimp. I need to appear strong. A few minutes later, Rose comes out the door and walks to my car like nothing happened. I follow her lead and continue throughout the day as normal. At the end of our time together I remind her, "Tomorrow I'm going to come pick you up again. Make sure you remember to lock the dog up this time, please."

Throughout the day I tell Alex what happened, then Cody later in the night. Both times, I stick to the facts. "So, my client's dog tried to come at me today, but thankfully my client was able to drop down and block it with her body. Then she got the door closed, so it was all good." I don't tell anyone that I've been on the brink of a panic attack since I saw the dog in the window. I don't tell anyone that my mind has been replaying the image of the dog trying to come out of the door. I don't tell anyone that all I can hear is the growling whenever I close my eyes.

Journal Entry: I'm an anxious mess. I feel so off mentally and physically. I can't stop thinking about tomorrow. What if something happens again? What will I do this time? People have told me how to react now so will I do better if I'm attacked tomorrow?

The next morning, my anxiety is harder to hide. I can barely focus, and my legs won't stop bouncing as I'm sitting at my desk. I contemplate what I need to do with Rose. Is it okay to cancel? Should I ask someone else to pick her up instead of me? I decide I need to make a new policy for myself. Rose is the first to be informed. "Hey Rose! So last week I was attacked by a dog at a client's house and because of that, I don't feel comfortable going to the door at your house anymore due to the incident yesterday. When I get to your house today, I'll send you a text asking for you to come out. Is that okay?"

"Yes, that's fine. Thank you."

I tell Alex of my plan, which she gives her approval. I hint that I'm relieved and that everything is okay now. But I'm not okay.

Thought Log:

Rose won't come out of the house when you text. She's going to wait for you to open the car door and send the dog out to attack you.

I need to leave the office at 12:15pm. It's only 9am. I start writing notes for other clients. I can't focus. I am trying to make a master list of parks in the area. I can't get it done without staring off into space thinking of the danger I was about to be in. Finally, I admit defeat. I need to focus solely on myself. I pull up an ASMR video on my phone. Alex can tell something is off, so she asks what I'm watching. "I'm watching an ASMR video." I can see her confusion, so I continue. "It's this genre of videos that I've started to watch when I'm anxious. There's a ton of different types but this one is like someone acting like I'm right in front of them. She's talking to me about everything being okay and telling me to focus. It's literally the only thing I've found that will make the thoughts stop, even for a few seconds."

"Wow, that's pretty cool." Alex turns back to her work, so I turn my focus to my video. I stare intently at the girl in the video telling me it's going to be okay. Right as my mind starts to wander off, she taps on the screen telling me to focus. How does she know? My breath starts to slow down. For the first time since the incident yesterday, my body is starting to relax. The thoughts aren't as bad. It's a feeling I get so rarely. Seconds later my mind starts to wander again. I try to fight off the thoughts, but I can't.

Thought Log:

Enjoy it while you can, because you're not going to survive much longer.

I close my eyes and try to shake them off.

Thought Log:

Yesterday Rose sent you a message. She didn't forget to lock up the dog. She was telling you to leave her alone. By going back today, you're just being dumb.

Doug probably hates you now for having animal control sent to his house. I'm sure he's telling everyone how you ruined his life. Plus, you gave up on him because you couldn't stand the thought of going back to the house. Pathetic.

I squeeze my eyes shut as hard as I can. Every muscle in my body is starting to hurt from how tense I've become. I push out my chair and place my elbows on my knees with my hands on my head. *Why am I like this? Why can't I just be normal? Why am I so bro-* "FOCUS" I whip my head up to see the video is still playing. She pulls me back in. Once again, my breathing slows back down, my body becomes less tense, and the thoughts start to diminish. It's a process I end up going through five more times before it's finally time to leave.

I pull up to Rose's house and send her a text to come out. Meanwhile the dog is still at the window staring me down. Rose isn't answering my text. I shift my glance between the front door, the dog in the window and keep a lookout to make sure no one is coming up to my car. After ten minutes I send another message. Time continues to pass. I can't push down the panic anymore. I've waited too long. I send Cody a text, "So this client isn't coming out and I feel bad. I just can't get myself to go to the door."

Thought Log:

If you get out of this car, you're going to die. The dog is going to pounce on you and kill you.

I start to shake uncontrollably as I place my hand on my door handle. My breathing feels like it's about to stop completely. Images of being attacked by the dog consume my mind. I pull my arm back knowing that there is no way I can do it again. I can't live through another dog attack. Right then, Cody responds with the validation I need, "Don't go to the door. You told them to lock the dog up yesterday and they didn't. You did the right thing to make a new plan today. It's not your fault they aren't following through."

After waiting for twenty minutes with no sign of Rose, I pull away from the house. I barely make it to the next house over before I start hyperventilating. I turn the wrong way that goes the opposite direction of my office. My mind can't comprehend what I'm supposed to do. Pulling into a parking lot to turn around, I call Cody. As soon as he answers, every tear I've wanted to shed since the dog attack comes out. I struggle to form sentences "I... couldn't... do it!" I find a dead-end to pull over.

Thought Log:

Someone is going to sneak up to your car, see that you're vulnerable and try to grab you.

My head is on a constant swivel to make sure I'm safe. I barely hear Cody telling me to breathe because I'm too focused on someone sneaking up to my car. What if the cops pull up because I'm trespassing somehow? They're going to see me and try to hospitalize me. I need to be presentable if they end up coming. While wiping off my face I try to tell Cody what happened. "The dog was just in the window and wouldn't stop staring at me. It felt like he knew what he was going to do. He didn't get me yesterday, but today was the day."

Cody always knows how to handle me in moments like this. "It's okay. You shouldn't be expected to go to the door when you tell them to come outside. It's not your fault."

"I just feel like I let my client down because I couldn't just get over this stupid fear."

"It's a very valid fear. You had something bad happen to you not that long ago. It's okay not to be totally okay with dogs yet. Do you want me to come get you?" The tears are starting to dry, and my breathing is returning to normal. Cody has missed so much work for me that I can't be the cause of him leaving again.

"No, I'm okay. I don't want you to have to leave work again because of me. I'll just go back to work." I talk to him my whole drive back to my office. Looking in my rearview mirror every thirty seconds to make sure my face is starting to look normal. I need to be okay by the time I get back.

I talk with Julie upon my return to let her know about my panic attack. "Hey just so you know, I just had a bad panic attack at my last house. Yesterday, the dog tried to come out of the door because they forgot to lock it up. It really freaked me out and when I went back today, I just couldn't get out of my car. I've decided that I won't be entering any more houses with dogs that aren't locked up. I'll give them one chance to lock it up and if they don't, then I'm not going back there. I told my client this new rule this morning so we made a deal that she would come out when I pull up. She never did, so I didn't end up seeing her." I feel powerful for sticking up for myself. I'm proud that I finally voiced my opinions and needs.

Julie responds, "Why are you still struggling with this?" I want to scream. My heart starts to pound from pure anger. Every emotion I was finally letting myself feel was just invalidated with seven words. I realize that I'm too broken to be fixed. There's no point in trying.

Journal Entry: I don't even know what's going on anymore. I feel lost and confused about my own feelings. I can't do it. It's too much. I just want to fast forward. Actually, I want to rewind to when none of this happened. I don't want to have any of these memories. They're awful and no matter how much I act like they're not there, they still are. It still happened and I'll always have to go through these emotions. I'm done. I'm over it. It's not fair. I'd still be happy and in a good place if I wasn't attacked. I hate my legs and seeing them makes me want to erase it all.

The next day, Cody points out that I may need to schedule an emergency session with Wanda. I hate doing it because it makes me feel like a baby anytime I can't handle things on my own, but I know he's right. Panic attacks aren't common for me, so when I have them, they're a huge indicator that I'm not okay. They tell me that I need to get help right away or things are about to be bad, quick.

Wanda can squeeze me into her schedule later in the day. Sitting in the waiting room I feel like a failure. I fail at being a good social worker, a wife, a woman and a therapy client. My problems are taking up too much of everyone's time. It'd have been easier if I had just gone. Not dead, but not anywhere near them. They wouldn't be in as much pain if they didn't have to deal with me. I start to make a scenario of how to run away but Wanda interrupts me. "Andrea, I'm ready for you."

I walk Wanda through everything that has happened in the past couple days. I'm shaking while holding a rubber caterpillar fidget toy that I can't stop twirling around. I start to worry that I'm going to accidentally smack myself in the face in a minute.

"Andrea, I've never seen you this anxious." She's looking at the rubber caterpillar that I'm currently wrapping and unwrapping around my hand. I try to put it down but pick it right back up. I can't sit still.

"I just feel so lost. Everything has just changed, and I don't want it to. It sounds dumb, but I accepted that I would be paranoid for the rest of my life a long time ago. I was okay with knowing that I would live a scary, lonely life because that's all I'm used to. Now I'm being told that it's all wrong! Everything I do is unhealthy but so what? I don't care anymore. I miss the old me. I miss being anxious and scared. I don't know who I am anymore and the more this crap keeps happening, the more lost I feel." I feel out of breath. Finally, everything I've been holding back since I was diagnosed is out in the open.

"You are grieving your old life. It's completely normal. This is a huge change and it's okay to feel lost." *Is it though? I'm the one that goes above and beyond for everything so how am I supposed to live with myself if I can't be like that?* Wanda can tell that I'm not listening. "What are your thoughts about trying medication again?"

My body tenses up. *No. Not happening. I won't go through what I went through last time I tried medication.* "I don't know. The last medication I was on, I felt like I had no emotions. Plus, I had crazy dreams that were so vivid. I couldn't tell my dreams apart from reality sometimes. I always woke up so confused and out of sorts." The memories still haunt me. All they did was take away the physical symptoms of anxiety but added a multitude of other problems.

"There are other types of medications, and that one was for when you were diagnosed with anxiety, not OCD. This time we know your right diagnosis, so you can try a medication more suitable for it."

"Okay, I'll give it a try." I feel defeated. I thought I could handle this. I wanted to be the one that could amaze everyone at how fast I handled all these bad things. Even though Wanda has told me not to, I want to ace therapy. I never want to admit that I'm not doing okay, because that shows weakness. I'm used to feeling weak, but not showing it. I'm not ready to show it.

Chapter 6

Journal Entry: Well, it's time for meds. I've come a long way and have become much more self-aware, so it's not a bad thing. I can't believe I never realized how bad my paranoia and checking were. Apparently, I've never really thought about or discussed it before. I think it'll help though. I hope the meds will help with the anxiety and paranoia. It's been long enough.

After putting it off for a few days, I schedule a medication appointment with a new doctor. This doctor works more with mental health rather than just general health, so I'm hopeful I'll have better results. I just need to wait a couple weeks, then I'll finally see if medications are worth it. In the meantime, I'm visiting my parents today who still don't know about my OCD. They're aware that I'm in therapy and have anxiety, but that's it. Cody won't be coming along since he's helping his cousin with some house repairs, but he wishes me luck before we part ways.

Thought Log:

Made a scenario about my family not believing my diagnosis and thinking it's wrong.

I feel nervous during my drive to their house. I know they will accept me, because they always have. They've always been there for support and have shown how much they care. I think back to when I graduated both high school and college, my dad gave me a look that showed how proud he was of me. Both of my parents attended every band concert, basketball game, etc. growing up. They even came to multiple marching band and pep band shows I was in during my last year of college. My mom will sit on the phone with me for hours to let me ramble about nonsense until I feel better. Most of the time I don't even think she can understand what I'm saying, but she'll stay on until I'm done. Once, I was in the ER due to a bad side effect of a new medication and they rushed to be at my bedside. So, I know they would never turn against me in any way. My main worry is that they won't understand.

Our visit starts normally. My mom, dad and I are sitting at the dining room table at their house in our usual seating arrangement. I'm sitting across from my mom while my dad is at the head of the table to my left. I can't help but fidget with a pen that my mom ends up taking away from me since she can't stand the clicking noise. I look around for something else to fidget with, but I can't find anything before my dad asks about the dog bites. I pull out my phone to show them the most recent pictures that I took a couple days ago. I can tell they're in pain after seeing them. My mom speaks up first asking, "Did you ever hear back if the dog was up to date on its shots?"

"Yeah, I did after I called a few times trying to get a hold of someone from animal control. She was up to date on everything so thankfully I don't have to worry about rabies or anything."

"Good, I'm glad you don't have to worry about that at least. How have you been doing mentally with it all? Are you still going to therapy?"

I can feel my body tense up. It's either time to speak up or chicken out. "Um, it's going well. I'm still seeing Wanda every week or two." I pause to make my decision. My heart starts to beat faster, and I can't make eye contact. Why is this so hard? "I actually found out recently that I'm diagnosed with OCD and looking back, I've actually had it the majority of my life."

My mom speaks up while my dad nods his head. "Do you think that's the right diagnosis?"

"Yeah, I do. It's been hard to fully accept, but I know it's the correct one. It explains why I've always been so paranoid too, so I'm finally getting help for it."

"Well, whatever you need to do to help yourself." I nod but know I have more to admit.

"Yeah, I'm going to start a new medication too. I realize that I can't be off medications because it's just too much to deal with on my own."

"How does Cody feel about medications?" Why does it matter what he thinks or feels? He's always been supportive, but honestly, I don't care if he approves or not.

"He's supportive of whatever I need to do." And that was that. The subject gets changed soon after but that doesn't stop me from typing with my toes "how does Cody feel?" through the rest of the visit.

Journal Entry: Finally told my parents – yay me! They responded okay. I wish I could go more in depth about how I feel and what OCD really is, but maybe eventually I can do that. Right now, I'm just glad that I finally told them. I don't like holding things back, plus talking about it and telling people helps me process.

* * *

It's been a week since I told my parents about my OCD, and I still feel positive about it. I'm starting to learn more about my own mind and ready to move forward in my treatment. In my last session with Wanda, she asked if I wanted to start doing more specific work on my OCD. *Yes! Please help me understand how the heck to manage this!* We decided together that we will work on identifying my obsessions and compulsions. I tried to identify them on my own before walking into session today, but I can only come up with one: checking when paranoid. I have a feeling Wanda is going to challenge me today.

"Alright, Andrea, I have this workbook that we're going to start doing together. One of the first parts is identifying your obsessions and compulsions so let's start going through the obsessions. There are eight categories."

Contamination Obsessions: The fear of germs and contamination, oftentimes worry around contaminating others.

She lists ten types of obsessions, but I don't qualify for any of them. I've never been too worried about germs or contamination. I'm relieved as I feel like I just passed the first test.

Hoarding Obsessions: The inability to throw away any useless or worn-out possessions.

I watch so many shows about hoarding so immediately I know that's not a problem for me. My house is nowhere close to being in a hoard! Then she starts reading them off. "Saving useless items?"

"Well, I guess I do that sometimes. I mainly keep my clothes that I haven't worn in years because I figure maybe someday. Then that way if I ever need it or someone else needs it, then I'll be prepared." I see her check the box. Oh no.

"What about feeling uncomfortable with empty space?" My mind wanders to moving into our new house a few months back. I couldn't stand the empty spaces because I kept associating it with not having enough money to buy nice things. Now that our house is starting to have the spaces filled, I'm far less worried about not appearing financially stable. Dang! That means I have to say yes and watch her put a checkmark next to another one.

Thought Log:

You're going to grow up to be a hoarder and Cody will leave you.

Ordering Obsessions: Needing everything to be "just right."

Wanda continues to the next category, "This one is more well-known and can be more along the stereotypes of what OCD is. Do you ever become preoccupied with symmetry, aligning things just right or other things like perfect handwriting?"

I want nothing more than to say no. We're only in the third category and I can't handle how many things I've already said yes to. "Well yeah, probably. When I was a kid, I remember trying to train myself to write like the other kids. I was always changing how I wrote to make it 'be the best.' I also wear my watch on my right hand and people always ask about it. Ever since I started wearing my wedding ring, I can't stand having both on one arm. It even bothers me when other people have a ring and watch on the same arm. Is that OCD?"

"It's likely that it's the OCD, especially since it bothers you when other people wear both. It's the symmetry piece." At least I have an answer now when people ask why I wear my watch on the wrong side.

Religious Obsessions: The fear, worry and preoccupation with being punished for improper thoughts or breaking religious rules.

I already know about this one. "No, I don't have anything in this category. I'm not religious, so I don't worry too much about my thoughts or actions in that aspect." Finally, I win another category.

Body Image Obsessions: Worry about your physical defects.

Ever since I started dating Cody, my self-esteem has increased drastically. I know I'll pass this one too. However, as I look at Wanda, she has a look in her eyes that tells me differently. "Do you ever worry about a physical defect that others will notice and consider ugly?"

I start to rub my thighs. The dog bites are still swollen and haven't regained full feeling yet. They're hidden under my jeans, but I always know they're there. "Well, I don't think I did until I was attacked. Now I worry about them anytime they're visible to other people." Why does the attack always ruin everything?

Health Obsessions: Fear of having a catastrophic illness and/or fear you will be responsible for a loved one's illness.

"I fear for my health, but also other people's health. Whenever Cody is sick, I'm so paranoid that he's going to die." I remember one of my past thought logs. "One night I couldn't sleep because I had a headache, so I went to lay on the couch. My headache started to go away once I left our bedroom, so I was finally able to start falling asleep, but I was so paranoid that it was carbon monoxide poisoning, and that Cody was going to be dead. I was so scared that I had to go back to the bedroom and make sure he was still alive." No one knows how many times I've checked to make sure he's still breathing. Even thinking about something happening to him makes my eyes tear up and my body tense.

Aggressive Obsessions: Worry and fear of losing control.

Wanda is flying through these categories, "This next one is about an irrational fear of losing control, harming others, being responsible for some terrible accident, etc."

These are the obsessions I hide the most. Normally my fears revolve around me getting hurt. No one knows that sometimes my fears are my inability to control myself. I turn to look out the window. I don't want to admit the things I've thought about.

Thought Log:

Fear that Wanda will hospitalize me.

"Yes, I've had some thoughts like that." I will keep it short because I don't want to explain any further.

Wanda looks at me curiously when I don't expand my answer. "I want you to stand up and hold onto my iPad up in the air." I grab her iPad and can barely focus on what she's trying to talk to me about.

Thought Log:

You're going to drop this iPad on purpose. You're going to have to pay for a new one and find a new therapist.

Smash this iPad on the table. You've always wanted to do something like that, so now is the chance!

"Andrea?" I realize I'm still holding the iPad in the air. I didn't drop it, no matter how much my brain told me to do it. "What kind of thoughts were you having when you were holding it?"

"I wanted to drop it or smash it. I also thought about having to pay for it though and all the other consequences."

"I had you do that because I wanted to show you that you have control of your actions. Even if your mind is telling you to do something, you have control of yourself." I've never considered that. For so long, I've been defined by my thoughts. Maybe they're not so scary after all.

Miscellaneous Obsessions

This category really got me. Out of fourteen listed obsessions, I admit to eight. They all revolve around being perfect. I think back to when I was in college. My freshman year I made a four-year plan because I wanted to make sure I stayed on track. I was given so much praise for it and ever since I've wanted to chase that feeling. Eventually, I was able to turn my four-year plan into a three-year plan and graduate early. Oh man the praise I got for that. I felt powerful. I felt like I was one of the best. The feeling never stays long though. It seems these days I will go above and beyond on something for work and even when I'm receiving praise, I'm already disregarding it and planning my next big project. I don't want to make mistakes because the ripple effect can be astronomical. I just can't risk it.

"So, are there any other obsessions that we didn't list that you think should be added?"

I think for a while then realize there's another one I've had for years that I've never told anyone.

"I'm always worried that people can read my thoughts, especially people that have passed away. Sometimes I'll try to think of something different, but it never works. I'm scared that people will realize I'm this bad person with these terrible thoughts." Have I said too much? I've hidden them for so long. What are the risks now that I've exposed them?

"So, how did it feel to go through and recognize all of those obsessions?"

"I mean it doesn't feel great." I try to put on a half-smile, but I know it's pointless. It feels awful. "I never realized how many obsessions I had." What's even the point of this? I'm hopeless.

"Well next are the compulsion categories. Do you think you are ready to move on to identifying those?"

No. I don't want to know. "Sure, might as well."

"Alright there are seven categories, we'll go through them just like we did the obsessions."

Cleaning Compulsions: Excessive, illogical and uncontrollable cleaning of objects and/or oneself.

Wanda knows I sometimes clean when I'm stressed or anxious, but I don't think she knows how much. "I guess I can kind of become compulsive. Whenever I clean, I usually do a lot at once because I want to be a good wife." I'm too ashamed to say how bad things really are. I fidget with my hands while I type with my toes the word compulsive, over and over. Just play it off like it's no big deal. I shrug my shoulders as I say "I guess sometimes I do too much without taking care of myself. Sometimes I'll get so hungry that I start shaking or I won't use the bathroom until I'm completely done, even when I need to go bad."

"Why do you think you do that?"

"I don't really know. I just feel like I must get all the cleaning done or else I'm not good enough. Whenever people come over to our house, things are bad." I lock my eyes on a book on Wanda's shelf that's behind her. I don't want to make eye contact. "Last week some of Cody's friends came over. For hours before that I was trying to clean and make everything perfect. Cody was cooking and anytime he'd put a spatula on the counter or even a little food fell out of place, I'd go and clean it up. I felt like if it wasn't perfect, then I'd be judged and seen as not good enough by his friends." I pause as I start to relive the anxiety I was feeling that day. "I felt so nauseous because I couldn't stop telling myself that everything needed to be clean. I would start to relax then make myself get up and clean random things. I even cleaned our upstairs bathroom that is never used. I scrubbed it spotless in case someone happened to go up there. There was no way I could risk being seen as unclean."

"It sounds like it's difficult for you to stop yourself when you're cleaning. For homework, I want you to make some guidelines for yourself when you're about to clean. That way, you have some rules to help you avoid becoming compulsive." I nod my head. I'm scared that I'll fail, but maybe now I won't feel so sick every time I clean.

Checking Compulsions: Checking over and over, despite repeated confirmations.

Well, I already know I failed at this one. The only ones I don't say yes to are about harming myself and shutting doors repeatedly. I realize I'm a visual checker, that's how I've gotten away with it for so long. My compulsions are so hidden that no one can see them.

Hoarding Compulsions: Hoarding, saving and collecting useless possessions.

I'm done with this; I already feel crazy enough. "Yes, I already know I do this one to an extent. I keep things because I want to make sure I'm prepared later. Plus, the whole financial thing that I already said."

Repeating, Counting and Ordering Compulsions

"So, Andrea, this category entails things like reading, re-reading, writing and rewriting excessively. Do you ever do that?"

I push my glasses on top of my head, place my face in my palms and rub my eyes until they start to hurt. "Yes, anytime I send an email or get an email that has any kind of important information, I re-read it multiple times over the next couple days." My voice is muffled with my hands covering my face, but I don't care. I just want to disappear. "I always want to be sure that I didn't make a mistake or anything. I must ensure that I don't misinterpret what I'm reading so that there isn't any kind of terrible ripple effect." My mind wanders to the email I sent before coming to therapy. It was to another social worker about one of our mutual clients. I re-read it three times before coming to session and will likely continue to review it a few more in the upcoming days. I can't trust myself to respond appropriately.

Body Image Compulsions: Checking one's body for defects and/or attempting to hide defects.

Again, if it wasn't for these stupid dog bites, I'd be fine. I cover them up when I can, especially at work. If I could find a way to get rid of them, I would. They show weakness.

Health-Related Compulsions: Reassurance and checking to ensure one's health.

Wanda asks me about excessive concern and checking about my health. "Yep, I check to make sure I'm healthy quite a bit by looking up my symptoms online. Or I go the opposite direction and use hardcore avoidance if I know something is wrong. Nothing can go wrong if you don't know about it, right?"

"You know avoidance can be a compulsion too." I use avoidance literally all the time, for essentially every obsession I have. I'll just go ahead and add that to the list of 'crazy things Andrea does that makes sense to no one else' in my head.

Miscellaneous Compulsions

Wanda lets out a sigh, indicating that we have another big category coming up that I'm going to fail at. "Alright, this category is miscellaneous compulsions and the second to last one." Thank goodness we're almost done with this torture. "The first one is doing mental rituals like repeating good thoughts, which we already talked about that one, right?" I nod my head. "Alright, the second is seeking reassurance?" Wanda had me do a codependency test awhile back so we both know the answer to this one.

"Yes, I do that all the time with Cody. I'm always worried he'll be mad at me or the things I do will have some huge effect on him. I'm always apologizing or telling him things that I've done then apologize for them. He never even cares and is always reminding me that I don't need to apologize all the time."

"Does Cody ever make you feel like you need to apologize, or has he ever gotten mad at things you've said or done?"

Thought Log:

I'm a terrible wife. People think Cody is a bad husband because I'm so messed up.

"No, not at all."

We continue through the rest of the list with Wanda placing more and more checkmarks. I feel exhausted and broken all over again. On one hand it's nice to know how many OCD behaviors I do, but I never would've thought there would be so many. I thought I only had one or two to handle. Now, I have a whole list of things to overcome.

OCD-Related Compulsions:

There are only three compulsions on this list entailing hair pulling, self-mutilation and compulsive shopping. Finally, one category I was able to say no to.

Wanda has two offices, and this office is within walking distance to my job. After the session, I'm walking back to my office, feeling sad and tired. Plus, Wanda gave me the workbook to take with me, so I have no choice but to carry it in my arms since I don't have my backpack. I do my best to hide the cover with my hands, but it's next to impossible.

Thought Log:

People walking by are seeing your OCD workbook and thinking you're crazy.

I login to my support group after I get back to my desk and hide the workbook in my bag. I need some reassurance that I'm not alone. Scrolling through, I see references to different types of OCD that I wasn't aware even exist. One that shocks me is Pedophilia OCD. It entails obsessing that you're a pedophile, even when you absolutely are not one. There's so much stigma around it but it's not understood that they're not the person's desires. I did some research and found that obsessions are extra disturbing because they're not how the person actually feels. My heart starts to ache for how much pain and isolation any person with this type of OCD must be going through. How misunderstood and fearful they are to speak up. How can I be wallowing in my own self-pity about my OCD when I clearly don't have it as bad as other people? I've been able to continue working and live a relatively normal life. Also, I can tell people about my OCD with little fear that they will shame me. How is this not talked about? Why is no one talking about the fact that people are suffering in their own thoughts because they're too scared of the repercussions of talking about it?

Journal Entry: I can't believe how little I know. I need to educate myself in order to help others understand because if I don't understand, then no one will. Time to pull myself up and work through this.

It's been ten days since I scheduled my medication appointment, and the day is finally here. I'm sitting in the lobby, waiting for my appointment, when I have a flashback to the conversation I had with my mom yesterday about OCD. We were sitting in a parking lot after going out to eat. She started to ask me more questions about my OCD, and I did all I could to explain.

"Well, I have all sorts of obsessions, but the main one is fear that someone will hurt me. So, I'll check the doors, locks, alarms, and whatever else I have in place to make sure I feel safe."

"I feel like part of that is normal though, right? I mean, I check the locks when I'm home alone, but I think sometimes it's just because I forget if I locked them or not."

"Mine is different. I know I locked and checked things, but it doesn't matter. My mind convinces me that I didn't or that someone undid the locks." Right then an older couple walks behind our car. I start looking at them in the side mirror.

Thought Log:

Older couple walked behind the car, thought they'd come to the car to attack, kidnap then kill my mom and me.

They pass and we're safe. "So, an example of what my thoughts are like, see that couple that just walked behind the car?" I point towards the front of the parking lot and wait for my mom to nod her head. "When they walked past, all I could think about was the fact that they were going to come attack us somehow. That's how my mind works, all the time."

"Well, isn't being cautious a good thing?"

I put my head down and shrug my shoulders. Why does no one understand how bad things are? "Yeah, but mine is at an unhealthy level." Maybe if I explain other types of OCD that are more severe, that'll help. "I've been doing some research and have found out there's a ton of types of OCD that I wasn't aware of. One is called Pedophilia OCD, so they obsess over being a pedophile, even though they're not." I expect the same reaction I had. Heartbreak and empathy for the people that must endure that.

"Don't you think that if they're having those thoughts then maybe deep down, they're actually real?" At that moment, I knew there was no use in explaining anymore. I've done all I can. No one will ever truly understand how much control OCD has.

"Andrea?" I whip my head to the left to see a nurse with a clipboard. Looking around, I realize that I'm still in the waiting room at the doctor's office.

Walking back to meet my doctor, I think about all I've done to avoid this moment. I thought I could handle things on my own. I had already admitted defeat once when I started the first medication and was kicked in the butt. Now they want me to do it all over again. Besides, if the medication causes any weight gain or acne, I'm done. I've already admitted I need help; I won't accept losing any more control.

The doctor is sitting at his desk and greets me with a smile. I sit on the couch across from him and take in his office. He's new so it's still empty, but there are some encouraging pictures on the walls. He asks me about my diagnosis and what medications I've already tried. "Well, I was on Lexapro and had a pretty bad experience. I felt like all my emotions were gone so I didn't feel like myself at all. Also, my dreams were so vivid that it made it difficult to know what was real versus not real."

"Have you tried any other medication?"

"No, not yet. I'm really worried about the side effects though. It sounds weird but I'm so used to being anxious all the time that getting rid of it completely is just not something I want to do. It makes me who I am."

I can see him writing notes throughout the whole time I'm talking. Is he about to hospitalize me or something? "Okay and what are your obsessions and compulsions?"

Ugh, not this again. "My main compulsion is checking things out of fear that I'll be hurt. Plus, my therapist and I went through some lists and realized that I'm also a compulsive cleaner. There are a few others, but I think those are the main ones."

"Okay and how would you rank your depression?" Why is he asking about depression? I'm anxiety based.

"I don't really struggle with depression much. My therapist has had me do depression and anxiety testing before and I'm mainly anxiety based. Even the things I answered yes to for depression were more anxiety."

He gives me another smile, "That makes sense. Let's give Prozac a try."

Chapter 7

It's 9am and I'm lying in bed, staring at the bottle holding my new medicine that's sitting on our TV stand. Is this going to be the answer? How fast will I feel a difference? What if I don't feel any different? I shift my focus to staring at the ceiling. I need more time before I get up to face the day.

Journal Entry: The meds are going to help you. It's scary with the side effects, but you can always go off them or change if they're not right. It's going to be okay.

Cody walks into the bedroom to see if I'm okay. He knows I've been awake for a while but haven't left the bed yet. He comes to lay down next to me with a concerned look on his face. "Are you okay?"

"Yeah, I'm just scared to start this medication. Last time I had no sense of reality, and it was awful. I felt crazy and, in a fog, constantly."

"We can work through whatever happens." He pulls me in so I can rest my head on his shoulder. Deep down I know that part of the problem is that I'm scared to get rid of the anxiety again. Without anxiety, I don't feel like myself. Cody speaks up after a few minutes of me being lost in my thoughts, "I found a funny video of a dog pushing a brick earlier, do you want to see it?"

I can't help but smile and say, "Yeah, of course." Lately, I've been trying to watch more dog videos to work on decreasing my anxiety with them. Overall, I'm okay with dogs, but not the breed that attacked me. I still don't blame the dog or the breed, but it's still too hard to see the breed and not automatically relive the attack. Cody pulls up the video and it improves my mood immediately. "I wish we had a dog so I could take funny videos of it." We've always planned to adopt a dog from a shelter once we moved into a house, but the dog attack really pushed it back. I don't know what I can handle right now.

Cody looks at me with happiness, but also surprise. He absolutely loves dogs. "Do you think you'd be okay with a dog?"

"Well, I think it'd have to be a puppy. I need to know that our dog is trained our way and we don't have to worry about behaviors or a bad history. Plus, it must be a breed that doesn't have any negative stereotypes. I can't help but believe them and I know I won't be able to change my mind."

"How do you think you'll do with things like taking the puppy outside at night or going on walks?"

My anxiety increases at the thought of standing outside in the dark or walking around town. Those are the most vulnerable situations to be in. I can't handle that. "I'm not sure. I think I'll have to build up to things like that. I'll need you to be patient with me and help me with things, even if they seem irrational."

"What if we start going on walks before we get the dog to practice?" Cody has been one of the most accepting people through all of this. Early on in my OCD diagnosis, I told him that he's more than welcome to talk to anyone he needs about everything. I don't want him to feel like he can't talk to anyone and go through this alone. He's my rock, but I want to ensure he has the support he needs if I can't provide it for him.

"I like that idea. Do you want to go for one now?" I get up to get dressed. I'm ready to work on this.

Thought Log:

You're either going to be attacked by a dog or kidnapped by someone. Cody won't be able to do anything to save you.

Cody and I make our way through parts of our town that we haven't seen yet. We talk about all the houses, what we like versus don't like. My anxiety is low when he's by my side until I hear a dog chain.

Thought Log:

Heard a dog chain, visualized I would be attacked and killed.

I look all around to figure out where it came from. Cody heard it too and can tell I'm struggling. He finds the dog first and points it out. It's on a leash in someone's yard. He tries to make me feel better, "It's locked up, it can't get to us."

"No, the leash doesn't stop them. It didn't stop the other one." I reach down to my right thigh where one of the dog bites is hiding under my jeans. Nothing is safe and the world has proven that. Cody puts his hand on the middle of my back. I look over to him and take a deep breath. He gives me a look to tell me that he will never let anything happen to me. I didn't even realize it, but I had stopped walking once I heard the dog chain. I give Cody a nod and tell him, "Okay let's keep going."

After the dog chain incident, we continuously hear dogs barking inside houses or in their yards. Each time I fight off the urge to run away, but each time Cody puts his hand on my back to let me know it's okay. I stop looking for the source of the barking because he starts doing it for me. Twenty minutes later, we made it back to our house. I'm almost amazed that we made it back in one piece. Maybe I can overcome this dog thing.

The rest of the day and the next day I decide to take a break from any type of exposure therapy or treatment for my OCD. I need time to rest my brain in order to fully process our walk. I've learned that rushing things just makes it worse. Throughout each day I watch a lot of ASMR videos, journal and laugh at funny dog videos. Cody pulls up some shelter websites in order to look through the dogs that are available. I'm able to look for short amounts of time but take breaks when I need. We'll find our puppy soon enough.

Journal Entry: I hate that I'm so afraid of dogs on such an extreme level now. I feared everything else, so why did dogs have to be added to the list? I already know that I'm going to have to do a lot of exposure therapy in order to get better. It's going to be painful and likely come with a lot of tears, but I'll be okay.

It's Monday morning and I feel rejuvenated from all the self-care I did over the weekend, but also stressed from the unknown that comes with being a social worker. Additionally, it's day three of taking my new medication and I feel no difference. I know I need to give it time, but I'm an all or nothing thinker. I like immediate results or none.

It takes me a while, but finally I work up the energy to start getting ready for the day. Cody has already left for work, so I go through my morning routine. My checking has decreased, but it's still there. First, I check the bedroom lock and behind the bathroom door before showering. Lock the bathroom door, play music, and keep an eye on the bathroom lock to make sure it stays locked. Once done, open the bathroom door, ready to put up a fight for whoever snuck in the house and is waiting to attack. Thankfully, no one is waiting today so I can get dressed. I take my medication and get out of the house. Another day safe.

When I get to work thirty minutes later, I decide to complete my therapy homework from last week. I have some time to kill, so might as well get it done. Wanda assigned me to make some guidelines about my cleaning to make sure I don't get compulsive. It takes me a while, but I end up with some good rules.

1. Do a check-in before starting to clean. If your anxiety is a 3 out of 10 or below, then go ahead. If it's a 4 or higher, use a coping skill (watch an ASMR video, journal, or play with a fidget toy) to calm down first.

2. Make sure physical needs are met such as going to the bathroom and eating if needed.

3. If Cody is gone and I'm feeling anxious, slow down and do a coping skill before any cleaning to make sure it's not a compulsion.

4. Complete normal chores first such as picking up around the house, dishes and laundry as needed. Do another check-in before any extra chores are done.

5. Extra chores include sweeping, vacuuming, dusting, cleaning bathrooms, wiping counters, and cleaning the stove and

microwave. If Cody is gone, only two can be done in a row at a time before a thirty-minute break needs to be taken. Additional chores can be continued after the break if another check-in is completed.

6. If Cody is home, then more chores can be done if the check-in is completed, and the anxiety score is low enough.

I feel good about this. It's simple enough to follow, plus I feel like Wanda will be proud of me. I'm going to hang it up on our fridge when I get home, so I won't forget. Also, that way Cody can see it to make sure I'm following the rules. After I re-read my list a few times, I put it in my bag to make sure I don't forget to take it home.

Going back into work-mode I look at the time and it's almost 10am. I have a meeting at the courthouse at 10:45am, so I need to get ready. Today is a little colder, so I contemplate which route to take. I can use the skywalk, which is obviously a lot warmer, but I'm always afraid less people are available to help me if someone attacks. On the other hand, if I walk outside, then there is more likelihood I'll be attacked, but more people are around to help.

Once I step outside, I decide to walk the skywalks because it's already too cold for my liking. I make my way up the stairs in the first building with my head on a swivel. So far it feels okay and all the people I see seem to look relatively safe. I decide to do some exposure therapy and put in my headphones. My anxiety immediately increases, but I tell myself that it's part of the test. I always depend on being able to hear if someone is coming up to me or about to attack. This way, I can use my coping skill of listening to music, but also learn to trust my other instincts to keep myself safe. I pull my water bottle out of the side pocket of my backpack so I can hold it to use as a weapon if needed.

Thought Log:

Guy is coming out of a construction zone with a board, thinking he's going to hit me over the head with it, flinching at the thought.

Passed a woman and man, thinking the woman would approach first to make me trust her then give me over to the man to assault me.

Guy catcalled me, worried about him following me to hurt me.

These exposure exercises suck, but I know doing them is the only way I'll get better. By the time I get to the courthouse, I feel empowered. I was anxious during the walk, but I also kept my headphones on the whole time. It feels minor, but it also feels major. It's something I never thought I would be able to do. Last week I challenged myself to sit in my car after I pulled into the garage after work, instead of running out of the garage immediately like I usually do. I documented how I felt throughout the whole time.

Journal Entry: My body feels tense, and I can't stop flinching while looking around. I feel like someone is about to grab my neck from the backseat of my car. I'm timing to see how long I'm able to sit here without letting my anxiety get too high that I go into flight mode. I need to go through this in order to get better. No one is here to hurt me. I'm safe.

In the end, I was able to sit in my car for five minutes before I felt my anxiety getting too high. I do my best not to minimize these accomplishments, but it's hard not to. These things are developmental phases I feel I should have reached when I was a child, not in my twenties. I'm behind in so many areas, but I'm trying my best to get where I'm supposed to be.

After my meeting at the courthouse, I decide to do the same exposure exercise on the walk back to my office. This time, it's easier. I'm still making plans on how to escape throughout the whole walk, but I feel hopeful that I'll get the help I need if I were attacked. It's a feeling that I don't get often as I mainly end my paranoid thoughts with me brutally hurt. Maybe I am getting better, but for some reassurance, I'm going to go to my in-person support group today. No matter what, they always provide praise and find the positives in any situation. That's what I need right now.

Journal Entry: I did it! I'm starting to feel confident letting my other instincts protect me. I'm capable. I need to remember that.

I walk into group with a better mindset than any other group I've attended. I'm starting to feel more comfortable sharing my thoughts without worrying that someone will play into my fears. Upon my arrival, I see our facilitators this week are Amy and Rodney. I've met both before and they're two of my favorites. Seated on the left side of the table is someone I've never seen. From the conversation between her and the facilitators, it sounds like it's her first time at group. I always enjoy it when new people come to the group because I like hearing people's stories.

Group starts and there's five of us total, counting the facilitators. We all go around to give a quick summary about how things have been going recently. I discuss starting my new medication and the exposure activities I've been doing. After me is the new girl. The first thing she says is that she was recently diagnosed with OCD. I start to feel butterflies in my stomach. This is the first person I've met that has OCD. It's something I've been waiting for ever since I was diagnosed. I've met people online through my support group, but this feels more assuring. I try not to be too obvious about how excited I am when I say, "Not to sound weird, but when you said that you have OCD, I kind of got excited. You're the first person I've met with the same diagnosis which feels good to finally have someone to relate to." She doesn't seem as excited, but I remember what it's like right after being diagnosed. It's lonely, confusing and all around hard to comprehend. I don't take her reaction personally.

Later on she is given time to talk about whatever she wants. She talks about intrusive thoughts and how debilitating they can be. Another group member asks what they are. I'm about to speak up when Rodney responds. "They are thoughts in which you have no control over, oftentimes leading to compulsions in this case."

The girl with OCD turns to me to ask how often I have intrusive thoughts, to which I reply, "Generally all day, every day."

"What? That sounds terrible! How do you do it?"

I shrug my shoulders, "Honestly I've had them my whole life, so it's just something I'm used to." I'm not sure if my answer helps or hurts. I don't want her to worry about getting to my severity, but I also want her to know she's not alone. Another participant speaks up to ask where I work. "I work downtown as a social worker."

She looks shocked. "I've always thought people who work downtown were all happy business people with no mental health problems."

I let out a small chuckle. "Yeah, that's not at all the case. I know plenty of people that work downtown who are on some type of medication or in therapy for their mental health. It can happen to anyone. That's why it can be so hard to get help sometimes. You're seen as doing okay because of these factors that make you appear high functioning, but you're not okay." I wonder if that sounds snotty or like I'm bragging about being high functioning, but I'm not. Some days I wish I fit the stereotypes of having a mental illness because I feel like I would get more support and empathy. Oftentimes I'm given different treatment since people assume I can just handle it on my own. That's not the case. At this point my right leg is bouncing uncontrollably and my hands are tensed into fists. All I can think about is the dog attack. How people reacted and how people are still reacting to me. I'm not sad or grieving anymore. Now I'm just angry.

Amy turns to me when she realizes my demeanor has changed. "Andrea, do you want some time to talk about anything?"

She barely gets the words out before I speak up. "Yes. I know it's been a while since it happened, but I'm still angry about the dog attack. People still ask me about the dog bites and honestly, it makes me feel like crap every time. I know I should be grateful that they care, but it's hard because generally it leads to them telling me how cautious they are around dogs now. I'm sorry, but I just see that as them benefiting from my trauma. Why do I have to go through this while they are able to use my experience to protect themselves? I sound selfish and I feel like it, but I can't help it. I never want to admit how I feel about this to people because the few people I've told look at me like I'm an awful person. Of course, I don't want anyone to get hurt but can you really blame me? I'm scarred for life! In fact, the other day I was wearing shorts when I looked down and realized there was a freaking dent in my left leg from the dog bite. It's probably not noticeable to other people, but I know it's there." I rub my hand along my left thigh to feel the dent. Before when it was just the scar, it felt like a cosmetic burden. Now that my leg's shape and structure has changed, it hits me differently. It feels like a whole new level of emotional scarring. "It's just not fair." I say in a whisper to mainly myself.

"I'd be angry too. It's a terrible thing that happened to you and it's hard when other people don't understand what you're going through. You're not selfish or an awful person." Rodney always knows what to say, that's why I like it when he's facilitating.

"I'm just tired of the fact that everything has changed. Yes, I'm getting healthier, but sometimes it doesn't even feel worth it. It's hard to explain because again, I don't want to be seen as selfish or ungrateful for all the support and help I've gotten. It's just exhausting to constantly be examining your thought process and changing the things that are unhealthy." I look at the other girl with OCD. I'm angry at myself for letting that all out. I don't want her to give up on her treatment. "I mean, I know it's worth it, it's just hard to handle sometimes." I don't know what else to say to make it any better. In a matter of an hour, I went from feeling empowered to feeling broken. It's a common cycle that I've grown accustomed to, so I know eventually, I'll get back to the empowered side. It just takes time.

Chapter 8

Journal Entry: It's been almost a month and I still don't feel any difference from my new medication. All the anxiety is still there as well as the intrusive thoughts. The only progress I've been able to make has been based on exposure activities and therapy. Maybe I'm just not meant to be on medications. We've been doing all we can to prepare for getting a dog. We haven't found one yet, but we know I need to work on things. We've been doing more walks and I try to do exposure exercises every couple of days. For the most part, they've gone well but there have been some failures. I know at times I'm letting myself fall into compulsions because I'm too tired to control them. Some days I like to embrace the OCD to feel the comfort of my old life. Other days I want to scream that things aren't improving fast enough. I'm trying to stay hopeful that I will find a medication that works for me, but it's not always possible. Maybe I'm too far gone.

It's a Sunday around 11am when I notice Cody is glued to his phone. We're laying on the couch watching TV, but I realize he hasn't looked at the screen once for the past twenty minutes. I ask him what he's doing when he turns to me with an excited look on his face. He shows me that he found a shelter that has crossbreed puppies that are a Golden Retriever and German Shepard mix. Immediately I fall in love with a puppy named Billy. He's pictured in someone's arms with the sweetest little face. Cody likes one named Ben and I try to get on board, but there's something about Billy. I can already picture running around with him and feeling protected when Cody isn't home. Cody can tell how excited I am when I can't stop looking at Billy's picture. He agrees that Billy is the best choice for us. We start to fill out the application with anticipation growing as well as fear of the unknown.

Thought Log:

What if we don't train him well enough and he attacks me when he's older? What if he attacks our future kids or someone else?

I push the thoughts down as we finish the application. We are required to take pictures of our house, so I follow Cody around while he walks to different rooms for pictures and then outside. I'm concerned about the fact that we haven't installed our fence yet. "Cody, do you think they're going to turn us down since we don't have a fence in the backyard?"

Cody doesn't seem to be too concerned, or at least he's not showing it. "I think we'll be fine. Besides, we can write in the application that we are going to install one. We need to wait for good weather." That means we'll have to have Billy on a leash or a lead like the dog that attacked me until the fence is installed.

Thought Log:

Made a scenario about Billy being on a lead in the front yard and attacking people walking by.

After completing the application, the automatic response we receive states it can take up to a week before we hear back. Once approved, we need to do a shelter visit prior to completing the adoption paperwork. I can barely hold back my excitement while we wait for our approval. This could be the solution I've been waiting for.

Journal Entry: I'm so excited for the puppy since we've been planning to get a dog for so long. But what if I'm not able to handle it? I feel like I'm doing better around dogs, but I never really know. I don't want something to happen that we must give him up and ruin his life. Just keep using self-care and practicing exposure therapy. It'll all be okay.

Throughout the next couple days of work, my mind is in a constant fog. All I want is to know if we can get Billy or not. I've been trying so hard to feel comfortable around dogs and the thought of not being approved already breaks my heart. I can feel that this is what I need. Billy could be the answer to my OCD treatment. When I was younger, and there were no adults around, the only time I felt calm was when I was babysitting my nephew. Even when he was only a few years old, I had the confidence to walk around the house when it was just him and me. It felt like I was his protector, so I had no choice but to be calm and confident. Once we were outside together when a dog came up to my nephew growling, so I stepped in front of him. He's like a brother to me and I would never be able to forgive myself if something happened to him. I'm hoping that when we get Billy, I'll have the same feeling. Then as he gets older, maybe he can become the protector.

I do my best to pull myself out of the fog when it's time to walk down to the courthouse again for a new client meeting. Lately I've been doing well with my exposure activities on my walks there and back. Sometimes if I'm feeling confident, I'll walk outside with my headphones in. Other times, like today, I take the skywalk but still listen to music with my headphones. Alex tested out a new route, one that takes you through more businesses rather than common places. It feels safer, so that's my go to route now.

Once I get down to the courthouse, I'm worried about the fact that I won't be able to receive any messages. What if Cody heard back about Billy and I can't get the message? This building is notorious for awful phone connections so I'm constantly checking my connection. Around the fifth check, I get the message. "We got approved to get Billy!" I can't hold back my excitement when I look at one of my coworkers to say, "I just found out that my husband and I were approved to adopt a puppy."

"Wow, that's awesome! What kind of dog is it?"

"What?" I barely heard his response since I was still staring at the message from Cody. "Oh, it's a mix between a German Shepard and a Golden Retriever. His name is Billy."

"I don't think I've heard of that mix before, but it sounds like it'd be a good pairing. When will you get him?"

"I'm not sure yet. We are required to do a visit first, finalize the adoption, then we can pick him up in a month or two when he's old enough." It feels like everything is falling into place. Not only is this going to be helpful for my exposure to dogs, but Cody will finally have a dog again.

Thought Log:

Billy will grow up to be violent and hurt you.

You will always fear dogs, even Billy. Cody will have to do everything to take care of him because you'll be too scared.

I do my best to push out the bad thoughts, but I'm struggling. On the outside, I'm practically bouncing off the walls with excitement, but inside I'm filled with anxiety. The contradicting thoughts never leave my mind as the next few days pass.

Journal Entry: I can't stop thinking about being hurt by another dog. I feel like it's just destined to happen to me. I just want the paranoia to stop.

It's finally Friday. Cody and I are ready to go make Billy's adoption final. It's a two-hour drive to the shelter. The whole way Cody and I can't stop talking about what to expect when we get there. Will we get to hold him? What if he's already been adopted and we must pick another one from the litter? The shelter staff told us they can't hold him until we pay the adoption fee. I can't help but wonder, if we can't get Billy, should we even think about adopting one of the other puppies? None of the other ones feel right.

Cody turns down the radio, "So how do you think you'll do at the shelter? There may be some dogs running around and barking."

"I mean I think I'll be okay, but I really don't know. Just keep an eye out for me, okay?"

Cody reaches over from the driver seat to put his hand on my thigh. He gives me a comforting smile. "Of course."

I haven't thought much about the other dogs at the shelter. Thinking back, I don't know if I've ever been to an animal shelter, so I don't know what to expect. Is there a chance that I'll be attacked again?

Thought Log:

You'll get attacked, freak out, then they won't adopt to you because they'll see how sick you really are.

We noted in the application that I was attacked by a dog because there was a question around how comfortable we are around dogs. I can't let it affect getting Billy. I'd never forgive myself. After grabbing Cody's hand that's still on my thigh, I speak up with my concern. "Do you think they'll ask any questions about the dog attack and how I've reacted?"

Cody shrugs his shoulders, "I don't know. They might but I don't think it would affect us getting Billy. We've been working on it."

Right then, I realize we are only fifteen minutes away from the shelter. The dog bite on my left leg starts to hurt. It feels like someone is stabbing a knife into the bite and turning it in circles. I try to massage it to make the pain less, but it's not working. All I can do is laugh at the timing. "Wow my dog bite just started shooting pain through my thigh. Think that's a sign?"

Cody laughs too, "It might be. It knows where we're headed."

Thought Log:

Turn around. Something bad is about to happen. We're trying to warn you.

We pull up to the shelter and immediately hear dogs barking from their outside kennels. I close my eyes and put my head down. I try to tell myself that it's okay. The fences are too high for them to get out.

Thought Log:

You've seen the videos. Some dogs can climb and get over fences like that. You're not safe.

Cody opens his car door then turns back to me. He can tell that the barking is getting to me. "Are you okay?"

"Yeah, I'm fine. I just want to make sure all the dogs are locked up and not able to get out of their kennels."

Cody and I both look around to see if there are any loose animals on the property. The shelter is in a small town surrounded by farmland. It honestly wouldn't be surprising if there were some animals roaming around out here, but so far, we can't see any. Finally, I let the excitement of seeing Billy overcome the fear that's keeping me in the car. We walk up to the office with Cody's hand on my back the whole time. He continues to check in with me to make sure my anxiety is staying at a manageable range as we walk past the barking dogs.

Once we make it into the office, it's a tiny space with another adopter standing at the desk. She's holding her new dog and is waiting to complete the rest of the paperwork. I smile at her, but also keep the dog in my peripheral vision. If it jumps out of her arms to attack, I must be ready. Soon a shelter staff notices us and offers to take us to see Billy's litter. She warns us that we can't touch him, but we can interact with his mom, Dora. In order to get to their kennel, we once again must walk outside and face all the barking dogs. At least this time we have a staff member with us. She's a tiny woman, but maybe she'll know how to keep us safe if one of them escapes.

When we get to the litter, we both let out an audible, "Aww they're adorable." In the kennel are eight puppies, but we can barely focus on them because Dora is trying to climb out of the kennel to be with us. We start to pet her and give her the love that she deserves. We remember seeing her on the shelter's website. She looks like a fox, so they must be careful of where they send her. They want to make sure she won't be hurt by someone thinking she's a wild animal. For some reason, I'm not afraid of her. I let her come close to my face with no worry she would bite me. It's a trusting feeling that I haven't felt in a long time.

The shelter staff pulls Cody and I out of our petting spree by picking up the puppy she thinks is Billy. They all have different colored collars on, but she didn't look to see which one was which. There's Billy who's primarily all golden, but there's another one, Brian, who is almost identical. She holds up both Billy and Brian so we can figure out which one we want. One dog has a green collar, the other is black. I get as close as I'm allowed and stare at their faces. I can't mess this up. "Okay, I think the green one is Billy. The other one's face looks a little different than the pictures."

"Are you sure?" Cody is smiling because he knows that really it doesn't matter which one we get, but he knows how important Billy is to me already.

I give them another look. I really have no clue which one is which. "If we pick the wrong one, could we still steal the name Billy for him?"

Cody is back to petting Dora when he responds with a laugh, "I mean yeah, we can do whatever we want for his name."

"Okay, I'm sticking with the green collar. That's my final answer." Cody stands up to put his arm around me for a hug. We stand for a minute longer to watch all the puppies run around and try to get a drink of milk from Dora's belly. She's still at the front of the kennel trying to get our attention again. Before we head back to the office, we give her some love with pets and kisses.

Stepping inside the office, the other adopter is still getting the final paperwork completed. We must wait for her to be done before we can get confirmation which dog we chose.

Thought Log:

You chose the wrong dog and naming him Billy would be awful. He'll never love you because he'll know he's not who you wanted.

After ten minutes of pure anxiety, the other adopter is done. We tell the staff at the desk that we're going with the green collared puppy from Dora's litter. She walks to the next room to look at the list of puppies and their collar colors. I hold my breath waiting to hear her footsteps coming back to the desk. "The green collar is Billy."

"Yes! Oh my gosh, that was so nerve racking not knowing which one it was."

Cody pulls me into a half hug, "Good job babe."

After a lot of paperwork and paying, we walk out with Billy's adoption finalized. We need to wait about a month before he's old enough to come home. Dora is still at the front of her kennel, so we walk over to give her another pet. If I hadn't been attacked a few months ago, maybe we could have considered adopting her instead.

Thought Log:

Dora is being left here and who knows where she will go. You could've adopted her if you wouldn't be such a baby about your legs. You just have to have a puppy.

Journal Entry: Dora could've been perfect, and Cody loved her too. It's okay though. I think he'll be just as happy with Billy. Hopefully nothing goes wrong with the adoption, and it all works out like normal. We've heard about puppies getting sick easily so I'm worried that will happen. I don't know how Cody would handle it if something were to happen to Billy.

* * *

It's been a week since we finalized Billy's adoption and I'm still battling with a mix of anxiety and excitement. Today I did a lot of exposure exercises throughout my workday. I've been doing all I can to get mentally healthy. Both to prepare for Billy, but also to prove to myself that I can get better. Even though I feel positive about the outcomes of my exposure exercises, I still feel exhausted. All I can think about is going home and sitting on the couch. I'm on the last stretch of my drive home from work, so I start to plan what I want to snack on before dinner. The road starts to curve up ahead, so I pull myself back into focus to watch my surroundings. I look to my left to see two children standing in a yard talking to each other. They look to be around ten years old with bikes in tow.

Thought Log:

Run them over.

I feel emotionless the rest of the drive home. I ponder what would have happened if I had done it. Their parents would likely have come out screaming when the cops came to arrest me. I would stay stone faced when the cops put me in handcuffs. I wouldn't try to run or explain what happened. I'd be scared, but it'd be okay. Cody would probably divorce me, but it'd be okay. My family would disown me, but it'd be okay. I would spend the rest of my life in jail, but it'd be okay.

Once I enter my house, I notice the counter has a few crumbs. I grab the cleaner to spray it when I realize the front of the microwave has some food splatters on it. After spraying every area, I get to work scrubbing.

Forty minutes later, the kitchen is clean. Another twenty minutes, the entire house is dusted. Thirty minutes later, everything is vacuumed. I'm sweating head to toe and shaking from hunger, feeling like I'm about to be sick. Looking around the house, I realize that I barely remember cleaning. It's as if my body just took over, taking all control. Did I do all of this because of the bad thought? I can't help but look at my cleaning guidelines on the fridge. I didn't follow any of them. I failed. Again.

Journal Entry: Why did I have that terrible thought today? Cody said that sometimes people have thoughts like that, and he knows I'd never do anything like that. I know that too, but this felt different. I had no emotion attached to it. Nothing mattered to me at that moment besides swerving to hit them. Plus, jail seemed perfectly ideal to me at that moment.

* * *

The next morning, I do my best to get yesterday out of my head. I have a medication check-up today, so I need to get it together. I can't risk the doctor thinking I need to be hospitalized. Although, I feel like I'm a fraud if I keep it to myself. I told Cody about it last night, but he knows me enough to know I'd never do it. I need another test with someone that will be honest with me. Turning around, I see Alex sitting at her desk on her phone. "Hey, I need to tell you about something weird that happened." She put down her phone and turned to me. "Yesterday when I was driving home, I was passing these kids in their yard and couldn't help but think to run them over." She raises her eyebrows, but other than that, no reaction. "It scared me because it was like I was emotionless as I thought about it. All I could think about was what would happen if I did it. Even then, all I cared about was that I would go to jail, which felt like what I wanted in that moment."

"That sounds scary. Is it something to do with your OCD? Like an intrusive thought or something?"

"Yeah, I think so. Plus, after that I went home and immediately cleaned like crazy. Like I had no control over what I was doing."

"Was it like you were manic?"

"Yes! That's exactly how it felt." Alex summed it up perfectly. How did I not realize it before? The bad thought made me so compulsive because I was trying to make up for it. My toes repeat the phrase 'manic' throughout the day leading up to my medication appointment.

Thought Log:

Don't tell the doctor about the thought. He'll hospitalize you and think you're a terrible person.

The doctor once again greets me with a smile when I walk into our appointment. "Well how are things going for you since we saw each other last?"

Should I tell him? "They're going okay. Honestly, I haven't felt much difference since I started this new medication. I still have the same number of paranoid thoughts. I'm doing a little better with compulsions, but that's because I've been doing a lot of exposure activities."

"And what about the anxiety?"

"No change in that either. It doesn't even really feel like the medication is doing anything."

"Okay, well maybe we can look at changing it to something else that is used more for OCD. Does that sound okay?"

For once, I feel excited. After the thoughts yesterday, I know that I need all the help I can get. "Yeah, sounds like a plan."

"Alright let me think about what I want to put you on, but first tell me what kind of thoughts you've been having?"

Earlier the nurse asked if I had thoughts about hurting anyone and I said no. Is this a test to see if I'll answer truthfully this time? "You know, the same as usual. Paranoid about people hurting me type things." He's quiet while he's writing notes. I squeeze my hands together as tight as I can, trying to work up courage. "Actually, yesterday I had a really bad thought about running some kids over with my car." He stops writing to look up at me. "Then afterwards when I got home, I became manic and couldn't stop cleaning. It was like I had no control."

"Have you ever been diagnosed with bipolar disorder?"

Wait, what? "No, it's never been brought up." He looks back at his notepad like what he just said was normal. Could I be Bipolar? I did use the word manic, which oftentimes is related to bipolar disorder, so maybe it was the wrong word choice. Or maybe my OCD diagnosis is wrong, and I need to be re-evaluated. On the outside, I continue conversing with the doctor like normal, but on the inside, I'm running around in circles, banging on the walls asking for answers while repeating the word Bipolar.

"Alright Andrea, I think we're going to try you on Effexor this time. It should help with obsessions and compulsions as well as some of the body tension and other physical symptoms. Does that sound okay?"

"Yep, sounds great." Does he realize what he's just done?

Thought Log:

You've been stupid the whole time. It's not OCD, you're Bipolar. Now people really won't want to be around you.

When I get to my car, I say to myself, "I'm not Bipolar. I know that's not right. I know I have OCD."

Thought Log:

No, you don't, you are Bipolar.

Chapter 9

"Hey Wanda," I smile when I see her walking through the door to grab me for our session. I haven't seen her in a couple weeks, so it's a relief to be back.

"Hey Andrea, how's it been going?" Wanda sits across from me next to her computer while I sit on the couch. I reach into my backpack to grab my homework. She had me list my helpers and the feelings I get when I am with them.

"It's alright, nothing too terrible." I respond while reaching to hand her my homework. She gives it a quick glance, then sets it on her desk.

"Cool, thanks. We'll go over that in a little bit. First, I want to get caught up and find out what's been going on since I last saw you."

"Well, we talked about how my last medication wasn't working for me, so they started me on a new one. I just started taking it so there are no big differences yet. Though I have been doing better overall with my OCD because I've been doing a ton of exposure activities. Oh, and we're getting a puppy!" I clasp my hands together in pure excitement. I can't help but tell everyone I see about Billy.

"Wow, that's nice!" She seems genuinely happy for me, but then I see the look in her eyes. She knows excitement isn't the only emotion I'm feeling. "How do you think you'll do with a dog?"

I hesitate to respond. What if all my progress goes away by admitting that I'm anxious about owning a dog? I've been doing better lately, and I don't want to risk being seen as unstable. "Um, I'm kind of all over the place with it. I'm excited, but still a little nervous."

"What are you most nervous about?"

"Mainly what he'll be like as he gets older. I know that we'll be training him and everything, but it's still scary not knowing what will happen. I don't want to be the dog owner dealing with a dog that bites people. I don't want my dog to affect someone like I was affected after my dog attack."

"That's a valid concern. I think it's a positive thing that you're thinking about those things. It likely means that you'll do all you can to make sure he's trained properly." I nod my head in response. "What about going on walks and things like that? I know you and Cody were working on exercises around that, right?"

"Right. I know that I won't be able to do it alone for a while. Cody and I have talked a lot about how I'm likely going to lean on him for support in taking the dog out at night, going on walks and all those other things that are affected by my OCD."

"Good, I'm glad you guys have been able to prepare and make those plans."

"Yeah, it was nice the other day Cody told me about this plan he has for me when we get him. He talked about how he'll go outside with me when we need to take Billy out at night. Then after I get more comfortable, he'll start letting me either go alone, while he's by the door or inside. Really whatever I need. It's nice and sweet of him to make a plan like that." I feel so loved and cared for when I talk about him.

"Cool. Has anything else been going on?"

Should I tell her what the doctor said? I really don't want my diagnosis to change again. I'm 99% sure I'm not Bipolar, but who knows. I didn't know I had OCD for twenty years, so can I really trust myself? "Well, something kind of weird did happen." I went on to explain the intrusive thought I had about running over the children and my cleaning compulsion afterwards. "I told my doctor about the whole thing and used the word manic to describe my cleaning compulsion. Right after I said it, he asked if I'd ever been diagnosed with bipolar disorder."

Without missing a beat, Wanda responds "No, you are not Bipolar. Please don't worry about that, because you're not."

I let out a sigh of relief. More than anything, I do not want to go through the emotional toll of another diagnosis. Wanda has known me for much longer than my doctor, so I trust her far more. If she says I'm not Bipolar, I'm going to believe her. "Okay I was pretty sure my OCD diagnosis was right, but you know me. It couldn't really leave my mind until I checked with you."

Wanda smiles back while looking at the clock. We're already halfway through the session, so it's time to look at my homework. I listed twenty-two people, the feelings I get when I am around them and the reasoning behind that feeling. One of the first on the list is older women in general. I added them for situations when I'm in public and need to seek help. I discuss the stereotypes I have in my head and how there is a comfort and a safe feeling around women in general. I feel disgusted by this because I know this is not the case. I know plenty of people, men included, that are just as safe, but it's hard for me to see that. Wanda continues through the list and stops to further discuss the specific coworkers I identified. I see them as an emotional support system for me because of the work we do. Recently a new staff member joined our office named Dre. At first, I thought we wouldn't get along, but so far, we've leaned on each other for a lot of support. I even took her for her first meal at my favorite burger place. Along with Dre, there is Joy. We've worked together on client cases and instantly clicked. The three of us have become a strong trio that prove to be supportive of each other in and outside of work. Finally, we make it through the list with Wanda impressed by my work. It always feels good to have confirmation about my good work.

"Alright Andrea, we only have a few minutes left, so let's talk about homework for your next session." Wanda looks at my helpers list then back at me. "I want you to look at your beliefs. Like what causes you to feel that men are so unsafe. Use this last assignment as a guide to figure out why you identified these people over others." Usually, I'm all for the homework she assigns, but this one I really don't want to do. It sounds like it's going to be painful to dig deep and identify the beliefs that have been ingrained in my brain for who knows how long. "Oh also I will be gone on vacation around the normal time you like to schedule, so do you want to come in a week early or a week later?"

"I feel like I can handle coming in a week later. I've been doing well lately."

"So that would put you out about a month, are you okay with that?"

I'm feeling optimistic in myself and abilities to cope so I respond, "Yeah, I think that's fine. Also, that will be right around the time we get Billy so it's probably a good thing to schedule after we get him."

Journal Entry: Things have been going well. I feel confident lately. I'm finally learning how to cope with everything and accepting my OCD. It still sucks at times, and I know I still have things to work on, but that's okay. I know I can do this. It just takes time.

* * *

It's been three weeks since I saw Wanda, and the day before we get to pick up Billy. I decide to work on my therapy homework, so I won't have to worry about it once we have him. After about an hour, I finished with fourteen beliefs. My mindset has gone from optimistic to pessimistic quickly.

1. Eye contact with men equals consent.
2. If you're outside in the dark, there's a guy watching and waiting to grab you.
3. Whenever you're walking or standing around any man, they're staring at your butt.
4. At night when driving on a dark road, if someone is behind you, it could be someone pretending to be a cop so they can pull you over and hurt you.
5. Life is full of traumatic events just waiting for one to happen. You're likely to have a car accident, death of a close one, illness, assault, etc. Likely multiple.
6. When others come over, if the house isn't clean enough, they will think I'm not good enough.

7. When home alone, someone knows.

8. As a female, I can't protect myself against men.

9. Even if doors are locked, someone can still easily get in.

10. As a female, someone will at least attempt to assault me in my life.

11. No matter how many security measures I put in place or how much checking I do, it won't matter, I'm still likely to have something happen to me.

12. I will lose my husband to an unexpected death at a young age.

13. If I don't clean up while my husband is gone, then I'm a bad wife.

14. My choices will always have a disastrous ripple effect.

Thought Log:

You're a terrible person. You have all these terrible beliefs. You shouldn't be working with people.

I re-read my list over and over. How can I say I'm an advocate and believe in gender equality if I think like this? I need to figure out what caused these things. I need to dig into my childhood. What caused me to be so scared and feel like I can't keep myself safe? Maybe it was the time a boy twisted my nipple at the swimming pool when I was in elementary. Afterwards I remember looking down and feeling disgust about my body. Or it could stem from when I was sixteen and a coworker who was in his fifties asked for my phone number. After I said no and told my direct supervisor, it was made into a joke instead of being taken seriously. Then when I told my parents, I immediately was told they would be driving me to work moving forward. Thankfully we were able to agree that I could still drive, I'd just have to walk with someone anytime I walked to my car at night. Maybe it's when I had an older coworker make numerous comments about my body while I was underage. For example, one time I was bent over the counter at work to talk to someone when he walked past and said, "I like that position." It could be the fact that like most girls I was taught how to hold my key in between my fingers while walking through a parking lot to protect myself. Additionally, self-defense has been pushed on me multiple times throughout my childhood and adulthood, but I've always resisted. It quickly became an avoidance compulsion because I figure if I learn the skills, then I'm destined to be attacked, right?

All these incidents help me understand how the thoughts started and grew to the proportion they are now. I never feel safe because I don't feel like I was given enough confirmation that I could handle things on my own. It felt like I was always being told how to defend myself with the help of another person. Also, it was proven that men could say whatever they wanted to me because I am inferior. I have zero confidence that I can handle myself if someone were to attack me, and that was proven when the dog attack happened. Afterwards, I was told how I could have responded differently, so obviously I'm not strong enough to do things on my own.

The more I think about the past, and these deep seeded beliefs, the more my heart breaks. I'm never going to get better. I pulled up an ASMR video to help calm the thoughts and start to journal.

Journal Entry: I need to start playing one of the ASMR videos whenever my mind is in a funk. It usually helps so much. I feel crappy about all the beliefs, but it's okay. This is part of growing. Wanda has been making me identify what I want to change, and this is part of it. I don't want to be like this anymore and in order to do that, I must think about the hard stuff. I must relive the crappy parts of life to finally process them. Everything will be fine. You'll get through it. Just keep pushing on like you have been, but it's also okay if you fall sometimes.

***

The next morning, I push all the bad thoughts out of my mind. It's the day of Billy's adoption and I just want to be happy. We picked up all his supplies after we visited the shelter for the first time, so we're prepared. We grab a towel, his new collar and a couple toys for the drive home. The plan is for Cody to drive while I hold Billy on my lap with the towel in case he pees.

After a long two-hour drive, and another thirty minutes of paperwork, we finish the adoption process. For the first time, I get to hold Billy in my arms. It was exciting at first, but quickly became terrifying when he wouldn't stop wiggling.

Thought Log:

You're going to drop him and they're going to take him back. Cody will hate you.

Shelter staff warn us to keep him safe, since he's so young, and still needs certain vaccines. They instruct us to keep him away from other dogs, since he's at risk for Parvo, which can be very deadly for puppies. I'll do anything in my power to keep him safe.

Thought Log:

You didn't clean your house good enough. It's probably riddled with germs and other things that are going to kill him.

The whole drive home, I know that I've already fallen in love. Cody and I play with him all night until he tuckers himself out. As soon as we put him in his kennel, he falls asleep.

Journal Entry: Billy is perfect. He's playful and cuddly and already seems so happy with us.

Bright and early the next morning, we have our local vet check him out. We want to make sure he's healthy and establish care with her. We quickly find out that he loves everyone at the vet and cuddles up to all of them. However, he also makes sure to come back and sit in between Cody and my feet occasionally. The vet laughs and speaks up, "Well it looks like he already knows that you're his people." She gives him a clean bill of health and it feels like we're in the clear.

After the vet, Cody leaves to watch a football game which means I get to play with Billy the whole day. I already know adopting him was the right decision. He already feels like my little buddy.

* * *

Around 2pm, I get a text from Cody, "I just heard from the shelter, one of the other puppies in Billy's litter tested positive for Parvo. They said we could bring him in, whether he's sick or not, so they can monitor him. If he is sick, then they'll give him the treatment for free. Is he acting okay?"

"Yeah, he's fine for right now, but what if something happens? What if he starts getting sick, what would we do?" I can't stand the thought of something happening to him. Although it has been such a short amount of time since we got him, the thought of losing him is too much to handle. He's running and playing in the living room, but I can't take my eyes off him. If I miss something and don't get him help, then I'd be the worst person alive. I'd never forgive myself for not saving him.

* * *

After a couple hours of watching him closely, I start to feel better. He's still walking around and playing, but then I realize that something seems different. He doesn't have the little skip in his step like normal. I know the walk he's doing. It's a walk filled with anxiety. A few minutes later he throws up. I console him and let him know that he's okay even though in my mind I've already lost hope. I want to break down, but I know I need to try to save him. Immediately, I call the vet hospital that's closest to us. "Hi, we just got our puppy, and he started throwing up. We were told earlier today that another puppy in his litter tested positive for Parvo, so we need to figure out what to do."

The staff member speaks up before I even get the final words out. "You need to get him here immediately." She says it in such a state of panic that I can't help but recognize how bad this could be. I try calling Cody but can't get a hold of him. I start to run around the house trying to figure out what I need to bring to the hospital. All the while I'm telling Billy that he'll be okay. As I'm getting into the car, Cody pulls up on his motorcycle.

"What's going on?"

"Billy just started getting sick. We need to take him to the hospital right now and get him help."

Cody looks concerned, but he does his best to stay calm. "Okay, let me call the shelter fast to see if we can take him there tonight." I anxiously wait in the car for him to be done on the phone. I'm not letting him die. He's going somewhere tonight, and it will either be the hospital or the shelter. He needs help. Cody walks up to the car and opens the passenger door. "Okay I can't get a hold of them. Do you want to wait till the morning, and we can bring him to the shelter so they can monitor him?"

"What if he can't make it through the night? I don't want to wait. I feel like he's sick."

"Okay, I'll go in with you." Cody closes the garage and jumps in the passenger seat.

As we head to the hospital, Billy continues to get sick. I sit quietly and barely react because I know he's going to test positive for Parvo. My hope for him to survive is starting to lower.

As we walk into the hospital, I hear one of the staff members at the desk say, "Uh oh," under her breath. I start to disconnect. They ask us to go to a room immediately. When we get there and put Billy on the ground, it's obvious how weak he's getting. He starts to dry heave. During the car ride he threw up three times, so he has nothing left in his stomach. He can only make it a few steps before he lays down and starts to fall asleep.

The doctor comes in to give him the test for Parvo. After what feels like eternity, she comes back in to give us the result, "I'm sorry, but, he's positive." My head drops to my hands. I'm already crying, knowing he's not going to make it. My little buddy that had given me so much confidence and unconditional love, is going to be taken away after less than twenty-four hours of being home. The doctor continues but I barely hear her. "You have three options. You can leave him here for the night to start treatment and see about taking him back to the shelter in the morning. Second is we can teach you how to give the medicine so you can administer it at home. Or the last option is to euthanize him." The last option tore through me. "I'm going to leave so you can discuss what you'd like to do."

Cody turns to me and asks, "What do you want to do?"

I have no hesitation. We're not abandoning him without doing all we can to save him. "We need to leave him here so they can help him if something happens during the night. I don't care how much it costs. Tomorrow, we can take him to the shelter so they can continue the treatment." We tell the doctor our decision.

"Okay we will start him on the medications tonight." Cody finishes up the paperwork and before leaving the room, the doctor tells us we can say goodbye to Billy. I take a last look at him sitting in the corner curled up. I can't do it. I have no hope that he will survive. I distance myself as much as possible. I walk out of the room knowing that was the last image I'll have of him.

Cody walks me to the front desk with his hand on my back. He asks me if I want to go to the car while he pays. Nodding my head, I walk out the front doors into the cold night. After pulling myself into the passenger seat of his truck, I lose all control. Every tear I had been holding back comes out. All I want is to scream at the world. I'm angry at the shelter. I'm angry at the doctors, but mainly I'm angry at myself for getting attached to him so quickly.

Thought Log:

You left him like he meant nothing to you! You're a terrible dog owner, wife and person.

Cody eventually makes it to the car and tells me about his goodbye to Billy. "When I went into the room, he was wagging his tail and was happy. I started to pet him, and he fell asleep on my leg. The nurse even walked in and said he's one of the healthiest puppies she's seen that has Parvo. Hopefully, that means he'll be okay since we caught it early. Also, the shelter called when I was paying, and they said we can bring him back tomorrow. I told the hospital staff to expect us in the morning." What he said has no effect on me. I have no hope. I'm already grieving Billy and the hope I had for ever getting better.

I cry the whole way home. When we finally make it back, I immediately walk to the bedroom. All his things are spread throughout the house, and I can't look at them. Already there are too many memories made in the last twenty-four hours. I'm already imagining having to box everything up. At least in the bedroom there's only his kennel and nothing else of his.

"You need to eat something for dinner," I look up to see Cody crawling into bed looking worried.

"I don't want to eat anything. All I want is to lay here and be sad."

"What if I at least make you some popcorn?" I accept it because I know how upset Cody gets when I don't eat. Sometimes, when my emotions are so big, I either eat a lot or nothing at all. Popcorn is usually the best bet to get me to eat no matter what I'm feeling. We watch TV while I do my best to avoid looking at Billy's kennel. I want nothing more than to put him in there to get ready for bed.

Journal Entry: I'm sad tonight. I'm sad Billy isn't around, and that we had to leave him at the hospital. I'm sad that he may not make it, or he will but then get sick again when he comes home. It's so heartbreaking to think he may already leave us so soon. It was so hard to see him shivering in the corner at the hospital and looking at us with those cute eyes. I feel awful for not saying goodbye, but I couldn't. I just had to get away. I hope when he sees us tomorrow, he freaks out and wags his little tail. I just want to be okay again and be able to do everything I thought we'd be able to do when he came to live with us. I miss him so much.

My biggest fear in picking Billy up the next morning is that he won't remember us. It has been less than twelve hours, but Cody warned me that he may be too sick or on too many medications to act like himself.

We pull up and wait by a side door as they instructed us to do last night. As soon as the nurse carries him out towards us, Billy shows excitement and knows exactly who we are. All the fear starts to decrease because we have our Billy back. I grab him and he starts trying to climb up my neck to lick my face. Even if we're not in the clear yet, he survived the night and he remembers us. At this point, that's all we can ask.

We make the two-hour drive back to the shelter while Billy goes back and forth between playing and falling asleep in my lap. I cuddle him as much as I can in case it's the last time I get to see him.

When we pull up to the shelter, Cody goes inside to make sure they are ready for us. A staff member has a towel ready to take him to their medical unit. He will be isolated because they can't risk spreading the disease to the rest of the shelter. They give us the same speech the hospital gave. "He looks better off than most puppies that have Parvo. However, there is still the chance that he won't wake up one day."

As we drive off, I'm filled with anger. There is no hope for him. He isn't coming back to us. Will we ever get another puppy? Our house now has a disease in it that can last for so long that we can't get another dog or else it could be killed too. I'd be a terrible person to even think about getting another dog. Billy won't even remember us if he does survive. He'll grow up thinking we don't care about him because I didn't protect him. I let him get sick. I followed every rule the shelter gave us, and I still failed. He's still dying.

Chapter 10

Journal Entry: I hope Billy comes back this week, but I also have mixed emotions when I want him to come home. We've received some positive updates, but I'm still skeptical of an early release from the shelter. What if he's not fully treated for the Parvo and this just keeps happening?

I'm in the worst headspace walking to therapy today. Each step becomes slower and slower. I can't help but just stare at the ground. I know I need to talk to Wanda about all of this, but really, I don't want to. I just want to be sad and wait for the inevitable call from the shelter to tell us he's dead.

Thought Log:

You're a terrible dog owner that caused this to happen.

After waiting in the lobby for a few minutes, Wanda calls me in. I don't say anything while keeping my head pointed to the ground. When I enter her office, I sit down on the couch and pull out my homework. I also want to avoid talking about what I've written about my beliefs.

"Alright, so how are things?" Wanda asks in a soft voice.

I take a deep breath, trying to hold back the tears. "Well, we got Billy last week." I pause to stare out the window. It hurts too much to say it out loud. "But then he got really sick the next day so he's back at the shelter getting treated."

"I'm sorry to hear that." We sit in silence for a minute while grief fills the room. "How have you been doing with it all?"

I let out a half chuckle, "Not well." I wish she still had the fidget toys out, but they're not here today. Without them, I play with my fingers, which eventually starts to make them hurt. "I'm just sad. I spent the whole day with him before he started to get sick. When he was at the hospital, I shut down completely. I acted like he wasn't even my dog because I couldn't even say goodbye." I can't help but be angry at myself for that decision. I let him down when he needed me the most. "I also feel like some people act like I shouldn't be this sad since we just got him. It's not like I want to be this sad. I'd give anything to feel better. Before we got him, Cody and I talked about if something like this were to happen. We thought that he would be the one to break down and not be able to handle it. How I'm reacting is way different than what I expected, but I just can't help it. All I can say is that I just want to be sad." I shrug my shoulders because that's all I'm feeling and thinking.

"It's perfectly okay to be sad about this. You are allowed to react and grieve however you want and need."

"I know. It's just hard because I'm so used to feeling anxious so when this overwhelming sadness takes over, I just don't know what to do. Anxiety I know and can handle. This stuff…" I hold my hand out towards my heart and chest, indicating all the feelings, "I don't know how to handle." I'm over it. I just want to sleep until this is all over. Is this what depression is like? If so, I don't want it. I'll take anxiety over depression any day.

Through most of the session, Wanda and I continue to work through my emotions about Billy and my expectations when he comes home. The one day he was home, I did okay with taking him outside at night. Cody came out with us, so I was still anxious, but I knew I was protected. We plan to keep up with the routine once things return to normal.

"Alright it's almost the end of the session, so let's review your homework. Explain what you've written." Wanda grabs her copy and starts to scan through.

"Well, I just thought about all the things that are underlying in my brain that cause me to be so paranoid. I realized that all the things I listed are things I've always believed. Most of them are things I've kind of conjured up on my own, but some derive from what other people have told me." I look down at my own copy. "Like number four, the one about if it's dark out and someone tries to pull you over, it's someone pretending to be a cop that wants to hurt you. I clearly remember being told if I ever get pulled over at night and can't tell if it's a police car, to call dispatch to check-in and try to get somewhere well lit. Ever since I was told that, it's just something that's stuck with me that I can't get past. Sometimes when I'm driving on a dark road, I get so paranoid and scared that I'll have to call Cody. I figure if something were to happen, then at least he's on the phone to hear me scream."

Wanda nods her head then takes another look at the paper. "What about the first one about eye contact with men equals consent. What are your thoughts about that one?"

"Yeah, that one really disturbs me. I don't know where that came from." I'm embarrassed to admit these beliefs to anyone, let alone Wanda. She's a strong, independent woman. What does she think of me now that it's clear I see myself as inferior to men? "I guess I always just try to avoid eye contact with guys anywhere I go. Anytime I pass one, I just put my head down or look straight ahead. I figure if I make eye contact, that will somehow send the signal that they're free to talk to me or do whatever else they want." I drop my head in pure disgust.

"How do you feel about these today? Do you think any of these beliefs are starting to decrease the further you go with your exposure therapy?"

I respond, but I'm barely focusing anymore. I'm tired and just want to move on with the day. Today has been filled with far too many emotions and talk about how my brain works in messed up ways. "Eh, I don't know. I think some of them I'm able to think through a little more and use reasoning, but other ones, I still struggle with a lot. I'm still hoping that if we get Billy back, that he'll help with those things."

Journal Entry: Well, no word on Billy, but I'm guessing he's okay. Cody will take care of it. He's just as concerned.

* * *

It's Thursday night and Cody gets the email. Billy can come home! If we can make the drive tomorrow, then he's free to go. I want to be excited, I really do, but I'm still so scared. I don't want to get my hopes up. The last time I did, it all came crashing down. One thing I do know is that we need to clean the house to make sure he's not exposed to anything bad that will make him sick again. I head to the kitchen to grab cleaning supplies when I catch a glimpse of my cleaning instructions. I read through them to make sure I don't break any.

1. Do a check-in before starting to clean. If your anxiety is a 3 out of 10 or below, then go ahead. If it's a 4 or higher, use a coping skill (watch an ASMR video, journal, or play with a fidget toy) to calm down first.

2. Make sure physical needs are met such as going to the bathroom and eating if needed.

3. If Cody is gone and I'm feeling anxious, slow down and do a coping skill before any cleaning to make sure it's not a compulsion.

4. Complete normal chores first such as picking up around the house, dishes and laundry as needed. Do another check-in before any extra chores are done.

5. Extra chores include sweeping, vacuuming, dusting, cleaning bathrooms, wiping counters, and cleaning the stove and microwave. If Cody is gone, only two can be done in a row at a time before a thirty-minute break needs to be taken. Additional chores can be continued after the break if another check-in is completed.

6. If Cody is home, then more chores can be done if the check-in is completed, and the anxiety score is low enough.

Alright step one, check-in on the anxiety. I'll rank it around a five, so I need to get it lower. I grab my phone, sit on the couch and turn on an ASMR video. I can feel my breathing get slower and my body relax. The anxiety starts to slip away. Twenty minutes later, I return to my list. This time my anxiety ranks two. Next, I check-in with my body. Everything feels good, I feel full and ready to move forward. Since Cody is here, I don't have to worry about the steps involving him being gone. I get to go ahead and start cleaning. I start with the kitchen in my normal routine. However, this is different than any other time I've cleaned. I don't feel the urge and need to clean. Instead, I feel calm. Throughout my cleaning routine, I do multiple check-ins, take breaks and routinely check my list to make sure I'm following each step.

Rather than feel an obsessive obligation to make sure everything is spotless, I feel a sense of freedom. For once, I'm in control.

Journal Entry: Tomorrow is the day, thank goodness! I'm still skeptical that he's fully better, but I'm glad I'll get to see him for myself again. I can't wait to do all the things we have planned for him. He's going to be so spoiled.

Waking up Friday morning, I feel more confidence in the fact that Billy is healthy. The test though will be to see if he remembers us still after being gone for a week. That will make or break me.

After what feels like ages of waiting, it's time to leave for the shelter. Once again, Cody drives while I sit in the passenger seat with a towel, collar and toys. We barely speak on the drive. We both have high hopes, but also fear of the unknown. By the time we get to the shelter, the dogs barking don't seem to bother me. All I can think of is getting to the office to see him.

"Hi, we're here to pick up Billy. How did he do?" Cody asks the person up front. She's been the person we've communicated the most with, so she will know best.

"Oh, he's been doing well. He's been eating like normal the whole time. We've tested him for Parvo a few times and he's always bouncing back and forth between positive and negative results. We had to wait until he had consecutive negative results in order to send him home. We've been thinking that he may not have had Parvo. We think it may have just been his immune system reacting poorly to the Parvo vaccine he got right before we released him to you last week."

Right when she finished speaking, another staff member brought him in. They put him in my arms, and once again, he went crazy. He remembers me. For the first time in a week, I feel like I can just enjoy this moment without fear. I look towards the staff who are smiling at Billy's energy. "Has he been like this the whole time he's been here?"

"Well, since he had to be in isolation all week, he didn't really get to cuddle up or be pet much. Unfortunately, he started to bite at himself too. Obviously, he didn't like it, so he's probably going to be a little clingy." That was fine with me. We protect each other.

The whole ride home and the rest of the night all he wants to do is play. It's constant running back and forth in the living room, chasing every toy we throw for him. Not once does he lay down until we put him in his kennel for the night. Before we even get in bed ourselves, he's asleep. I look at Cody and smile with tears in my eyes. "I'm so happy he's finally home."

"Me too babe." We hug, take one last look at him, and then crawl into bed.

Journal Entry: He's back and he remembers us. I'm so happy, I can't even hold back my excitement to have him back.

The past couple weeks of having Billy home have gone well. He hasn't shown any signs of being sick and doing well with the rules we've set for him. Since all seems to be going well, we decide to try our first walk. I know that I need Cody for this because I don't feel confident walking around alone just yet. I still don't know how I'll react to other dogs and with Billy, they'll be drawn to us.

After getting everything ready that we need, we set out. I'm holding the leash so Cody can help instruct me on what to do when Billy tries to pull. I feel like I'm getting the hang of it when I realize there's a loose dog up ahead. Billy and the dog spot each other as the other dog starts to come up to us. Everything starts to get fuzzy, and I can't hear what Cody is saying. I start to feel Billy tugging, so I grab the handle on his harness to hold him back. I try to see what's going on, but all I see is Cody with the other dog, trying to hold him back. I turn my head away and close my eyes.

Thought Log:

It's happening again. The dog is loose and you're going to be attacked. Even worse, Cody may be attacked, and you're not present enough to help him.

I do my best to focus back on what's happening, but it's still a blur. Suddenly, I feel Cody's hand on my back while he takes Billy's leash. "Hey, are you okay?"

I turn my head to see him come into focus. "Yeah, I think so." I look around to figure out where the other dog is.

Cody explains what happened. "Don't worry, the dog's owner came out and grabbed him. A little kid was out front with the dog when he ran over to us. The kid tried to grab onto it, but it was too big, so the dad came out when he realized what was going on."

"Oh okay, good." I keep looking around to get my mind right. We're in the middle of the road, Billy is still huffing at the dog that's no longer there, and Cody is looking at me with worried eyes. "I think I blacked out. It was like I couldn't see or hear anything going on. The growling and loose dog… it triggered something." I'm confused and scared. What if this had happened when I was alone?

"It's okay, you're safe." Cody pulls me close until I make eye contact with him. I take a deep breath then give him the nod that indicates we can move forward. Another bad situation put to rest.

Once we get home, I think about all that happened. I had no clue I would still react that strongly to dogs. I can't help but think about how little control I had of the situation. If Cody hadn't been there, I would have been vulnerable to all sorts of terrible things. Once again, I feel like my mind is just getting sicker, not better. I know I need to process this all, but right now I just want to ignore it. Also, I must put my focus elsewhere. Tonight is my night to make dinner, which I always hate. I'm always terrified I'll screw it up, which means I won't be a good enough wife for Cody. I've tried making things in the past, but I always fail. Once I wanted to make cookies from scratch for Christmas, so I made a practice batch first. They turned out great, so I set out to make them again the day of the Christmas party. I followed all the same instructions, but this time I decided to get new cookie sheets to bake them on. I didn't realize that the new sheets were different than my old ones and they burnt to a crisp. I had a mental breakdown. I was crying when Cody picked up his keys and headed to the door. When I asked where he was going, he responded "to fix this." He returned with a different type of cookie from a package so we could make it before the party. Ones that I was able to make without any problems.

Unfortunately, tonight I can't just make cookies or depend on Cody to make dinner like I do most nights. Tonight, I need to take care of him for once. To keep things easy, I choose to make macaroni and cheese, because I know I won't screw it up. I start boiling the water and notice Billy is standing below me wagging his tail.

Thought Log:

I should pour this boiling water on him.

I have no emotions attached to the thought. The consequences don't seem to matter. I stand there motionless as Billy starts to rub against my leg, asking to be pet. It pulls me back into reality and just like my intrusive thought about running over the kids, I start to spiral. Did I just think about killing him? Am I a monster? Is Cody going to leave me? Will I be hospitalized if anyone finds out? What if someone tries to take Billy? Does Billy know that I thought that and hate me now?

I lean down and hold Billy while trying to calm down. I whisper "I'm so sorry" to him over and over. Of course, he has no clue what's going on, but I know. He's going to love me unconditionally, but maybe he shouldn't. I don't deserve him.

Later in the night, I work up the courage to tell Cody. Just like before, I need confirmation that I'm not a terrible person. "I need to tell you something." Cody puts down his phone and turns to me. "Tonight, when I was making dinner, I thought about pouring the boiling water on Billy."

Cody makes a face that's hard to read. He looks shocked, but also that it's not too serious. "Obviously you wouldn't hurt him though." Was he asking a question or making a comment?

"No, of course not. It was just a crazy feeling, just like the last bad thought I had when I was driving. It just makes me feel bad." I look over to Billy who's chewing on his bone. I know it's just the OCD, but that doesn't make it any better. I'm a monster.

Chapter 11

Today is the day. Cody will be out of town for the first time in months. This is the first time I'll have Billy with me on one of these nights. It's the moment I've been waiting for to truly see how much progress I've made. Will I be able to sleep without a light on? What happens if I hear a noise, will I freak out as much as I used to? All I want is to solely focus on how I can make tonight work but instead, my mind is focused elsewhere.

Today I have a meeting with Dre, Joy, a couple coworkers and management to talk about some problems that have recently arisen. A few weeks back, Joy was assaulted by someone while walking through the skywalks to the courthouse. Thankfully she was able to get away, but not before the person injured her while trying to grab her. The aftermath for her has felt like my dog attack. She also had coworkers make inappropriate comments that only made things worse. Her boundaries weren't respected, even when they were clearly stated.

A week after the incident, there was an all staff meeting about the incident that was supposed to be structured around how to feel safe in the community. Instead, from my perspective, it turned into blaming, lack of accountability and both Joy and I walking out. I was attempting to speak up about how what was happening to Joy wasn't a one-time deal as I had dealt with it also. At a certain point, I lost it and left crying because I didn't feel heard, once again. Joy left because every time she attempted to speak up, someone spoke over her. All around, it was a meeting that would bring Joy, Dre and I closer together, but also feel isolated throughout the rest of the building. Before the meeting, I write in my journal to calm some anxiety.

Journal Entry: I'm so nervous. Part of me wants to continue this advocacy but part of me wants to ignore it. I'm so tired and defeated. I wish I had therapy this week. Hopefully Joy is okay, and I hope I can help rather than hurt.

After I finish journaling, I find Joy and Dre to pass out the donuts I brought so we all can eat our feelings. Dre speaks up first, "So Joy, how are you feeling going into this meeting?"

Joy lets out a laugh, "I mean I'm pretty sure I'm going to end up not being able to be heard and walk out, just like last time."

We all let out a chuckle, but unfortunately, we know it's true. We know there is a chance we all end up walking out over frustration and feeling overwhelmed. Joy has her safe person that has been speaking up for her when Joy isn't able to. Dre is that person for me. Overall, we're all protective of each other, especially of Joy since her accident was so recent. In the past, I tried to speak up about changes that needed to be made regarding a staff crisis, but I wasn't heard. Now we're making our voices be heard because I can't watch anyone else go through this. Work is somewhere that we're supposed to feel safe, especially since, as social workers, we pride ourselves on safety. Instead, it's turned into an anxiety provoking place, that as of late has been making me never want to leave my desk.

Looking at the time, it's only a couple minutes until our meeting. "Alright guys, are we ready for this?"

Dre and Joy both look over to me with slight nods, but also some uncertainty in their voices. In unison they say, "I guess."

After walking into the meeting room, we each sit next to our designated safe person. I come ready with a fidget toy, because I know I will need it. Joy and I asked for a neutral facilitator that didn't know any of the past situation, that way they could be impartial. The facilitator breaks the tension by discussing why we're all here. "Alright guys, we're having this meeting today because there's been some situations that we need to talk about, and how to respond to them better in the future. So, I believe we're going to focus mainly on safety today, but if other things come up, then we can look at having future meetings to continue talking out what needs to be done." Once everyone agrees and completes a feelings check-in, I speak up first.

"I'm just feeling frustrated with how everything went with my incident, and now Joy's incident. Ever since that all-staff meeting where we talked about safety, I feel like I'm going through my dog attack all over. I feel like I'm being re-traumatized by all of this because I still don't feel heard. It took me walking out of that meeting crying to really be listened to." I'm shaking with adrenaline mixed with anxiety. I'm not used to being so assertive when it comes to how I feel. It feels empowering, but also unknown and scary.

Joy starts to speak up and I'm proud of her. "Yes, I feel like all that's happened since I was hurt has just re-traumatized me and made things ten times worse. People have been reacting so weirdly to me. This place used to feel safe and now I dread coming here." There's an unsaid agreement that if anyone attempts to invalidate what Joy says, we will step in.

The meeting progresses well, but at one point I do step out to a room designated for self-care. Since this is work, I need to remain professional and in order to do that, I needed a break. Everything that's been going on has been so heartbreaking to watch. Not only seeing someone else go through something so traumatic, but also how it has affected my exposure therapy. I have been battling my own mind trying to figure out how I can be safe while using the skywalks.

Prior to Joy's incident, I thought the skywalks were the safest way to walk around. I was doing all my exposure activities using them because I felt that I was in a safe enough space. Now I don't know what's safe because I'm being told such conflicting information. Some people say to only walk outside now. Beforehand the skywalks were deemed safer than outside, so how can we switch it now? If I stop using the skywalks, is that an avoidance compulsion, or is it a rational response? I've been lost, confused and worried about my ability to make progress. Every time I walk to the courthouse, I worry that it's my time to die.

Even Cody has had anxiety about me walking around. The first time I had to use the skywalks after Joy's incident, we had a long talk the night before about what to do during the walk. For a while I was concerned that he would try to tell me I just couldn't use them anymore. It felt like a common response I was used to getting. Instead, he said he trusted me. He knows that I will make the right decision and to just trust my instincts. It was something I hadn't been told much in my life, but it was exactly what I needed. Rather than being told what to do, it's in my hands to keep myself safe.

Returning to the meeting, I feel better and less agitated. They've moved on to how we can address these things in the future. Many things are discussed but, in the end, we decide that in order to ensure everyone has a voice, we need a peer lead group focused on safety. Although our management is great, it seems that we often go to our coworkers for support. This group would revolve around staff that are up for advocacy and being that support person for anyone that may get hurt at work. I think back to all the therapy homework I've done. One that sticks out is my list of safe people I made. "You know, once in therapy I had to identify all my safe people. Instead of just generally saying 'this person is safe' I had to explain in what situations I go to them in. If it's only in a crisis, if it's about my relationship, mental health, work, family, etc. It really helped me understand how I saw the people in my life. Honestly, I think everyone should do it."

Dre was next to me with a proud look on her face. "Yeah, I agree. That way if someone doesn't want to come to this committee we're putting together, then they know right off hand who they can go to."

One of the managers speaks up, "What about management with this group, we still want to make sure they're in the loop."

My frustration level rises slightly. "We for sure want and need management to be involved because that's necessary. This is a way for the person that is hurt to go through one person rather than go through multiple people. Someone from the committee could be their advocate and speak with management and do regular check-ins. That way the person that's hurt or going through something traumatic can have their space and be less overwhelmed."

Something has been bothering me throughout both incidents and I think it could make an impact. "You know the things that have been done, and said, to Joy and I after our incidents, staff would never do to our clients. It's almost as if we lose our mental health backgrounds and ability to deal with crisis when it comes to our coworkers. It's not being recognized that trauma can affect everyone. Every employee here should know what's appropriate, versus not appropriate, but they need to be able to apply it to everyone, not just the clients. This committee is a way to ensure that buffer and protection for the hurt person."

Finally, after another twenty minutes, the meeting is over, and our committee is in the works. I feel my voice has finally been heard. Things may not be completely over, but at least I've done what I can.

Journal Entry: Well, I'm hopeful this processing chapter is over. I want to move forward. No more dwelling on the past. I can't do it anymore. I've proven my strength and abilities and that's all that matters. Go me!

* * *

Walking inside the house later that night, I push everything with work out of my mind. I try to focus on what's real versus what's not real. I lock the door and turn on the alarm like normal, but instead of checking the closet and bathroom, I walk right past them. I go to let out Billy from his kennel and immediately feel a sense of safety. I contemplate walking through the house, but I don't feel the urge or need to do it. I figure Billy will find them if someone is waiting inside to attack. Instead of doing the normal walk through, I let him outside, then change clothes. I don't tiptoe around or try to stay quiet. The curtains are left closed. After I turn on the TV, I sit on the couch instead of the chair. I don't feel the need to keep an eye on the doorway.

As it gets darker, I remain in the living room rather than go to bed. Instead, I go to bed when I'm tired, not just when I'm too scared to be in the other parts of the house. Heading into the bedroom, I don't feel the need to do any type of checking. I still lock the bedroom door, turn on the TV and the desk lamp. Billy is restless and struggling to fall asleep, I'm guessing since he's used to sleeping in the dark. I feel weirdly off and annoyed by the light rather than safe like I did in the past.

After an hour, I decide it's time to test something that I haven't done since elementary school. I turn off the TV, turn my phone flashlight on then turn the desk lamp off. I let myself adjust to the different lighting before deciding if I can turn the flashlight off.

Thought Log:

I thought someone was standing behind me, I resisted the urge to look.

Heard a noise, thought someone was breaking in, but figured since Billy wasn't panicking, it was okay.

The thoughts are all happening, but I'm not having the same reaction. My heart isn't racing, my hands are steady, rather than shaking, and my eyes aren't darting to the door lock. Slowly, I look down at the phone in my hands. Am I really ready for this? I've waited for this moment for so long and I'm scared to fail again. These past few months I've been working so hard. Even during the hard moments, I've still tried to complete exposure exercises because I know it will eventually be worth it. A recent session with Wanda pops into my mind.

"What's the point in trying to get better? Some days I wish I could go back to before I was even diagnosed with OCD and just keep living life how I was." I held my head down, avoiding eye contact. I paused to admit something that I didn't want to admit. "Lately I've just wanted to leave. I want to run away from all of this and just go do drugs or something. That way I can just get arrested, go to jail and not have to deal with any of this. I don't want to do this anymore. I don't want Cody or any of my family to have to go through this anymore."

Wanda gave me a sympathetic look. "What do you think your life would be like if you didn't have OCD?"

I thought long and hard before I responded. "If I didn't have OCD… my head wouldn't be filled with constant thoughts and the need to reach safety. I wouldn't be the butt of jokes about my paranoia. I would be more trusting in people because I wouldn't have the obsessions that they could hurt me in some way. I would feel like I could protect myself physically, mentally and emotionally. I would feel like I'm enough and that I don't have to feel crazy in order to be the best. I could experience things without the fear of embarrassment and failure. I could let things go and move on. I may have been able to avoid some negative relationships. I may have been more confident in jobs to assert myself and my needs due to having less fear of making others upset or less proud of me. I would get along better with people because I could be more of who I am and not only show the laughing side. I could walk around places like a normal person without the fear and the need to check constantly on my mind. I could sleep normally when I'm alone. I could make more friends without the fear of them being out for me somehow. I wouldn't have to celebrate such minor accomplishments that I should've mastered years ago like walking around outside after dark."

"You sound angry about what your life could've been."

"Of course, I'm angry! How did no one notice how messed up I was my entire childhood? Do you know how many times I didn't do things with my friends because I told myself I wouldn't be safe? Do you know how many plans I've canceled, because I thought even the choice of driving somewhere would cause a ripple effect of someone close to me dying? I slept on the floor in a sleeping bag for a year in high school because I was too scared to sleep in my bed!"

Wanda's next question made my heart hurt and guilt take over. "Who are you most angry with?"

"Well, most of the time I feel angry towards my parents" I looked down in shame as my eyes welled up. "Anytime they say they feel bad about it though, I take the blame. I should've said something. How am I supposed to expect anyone to notice when I hid it so well?"

"You were just a kid. How were you supposed to know what you were doing?"

"I don't know. I just don't want to hurt them, and I don't want them to blame themselves. Plus, how were they supposed to know?" I picked up a stress ball that was sitting on the table and started picking at it. "I want things to go back to normal."

I could feel Wanda watching me fidgeting before replying, "It sounds like you're experiencing some all-or-nothing thinking. Your brain is telling you that it's either you go all in to get better, or you completely go the other way."

"How can I be expected to completely change my way of thinking? I've had these ways of keeping me safe for twenty years. How am I supposed to just give them up?" Maybe that's what I was most angry about. I was being asked to change everything I've ever known.

"You learn how to trust yourself to keep yourself safe. You figure out how to feel okay with the unknown. You ask for help and depend on your safe people to help you through this."

I was filled with so much anger and wanted to live a different life during that session, but is that really what I want? I look around the room and think about all the positive things I have in my life. I made it to this point in my life even with the OCD. There's no point in fighting against it. I'm strong and I can protect myself, even if it's scary to think about.

I look down at my phone again and push the button that could change everything. It's officially dark. Initial panic makes my heart race, but it feels more like the response I should be having rather than how I truly feel. After my eyes adjust, I realize that I can see enough of the room to feel safe. I lay my head down on my pillow and cover up with the blanket. Even with my eyes open, I can't see the door like I normally can when I would position myself propped up and surprisingly, I'm okay with that. It feels like a whole new beginning and I'm ready for it.

Journal Entry: I feel independent, which is something I'm not used to, but it feels good. Hopefully things keep going well and smoothly. Finally, I'm going to sleep with the lights off!!

* * *

Waking up the next morning, I send Cody a text with pure excitement about my accomplishment. It feels small, and I feel silly celebrating, but I can't help it. It's another thing that I never thought I'd be able to do. Throughout the week, I tell my parents, coworkers and anyone else that will listen about what I did. Everyone that knows what I'm going through, understands how much progress that means I'm making. Rather than being seen as a scared, paranoid, codependent individual, I feel like I'm starting to be seen as strong, assertive and independent. It's everything I could have hoped for and never thought I would achieve.

Chapter 12

It's been a month since I started sleeping in the dark. It feels great, but also exhausting to be putting this much work into my mental health on a constant basis. Therefore, yesterday, I decided that I need to take a breather. I'm stressed and my body is telling me to take a break. Throughout my social work career, there have been only a few times I've taken breaks when I needed to. I usually ignore the signs and power through. It leads to burnouts, high anxiety, lack of sleep and acne. I can't keep doing this cycle. If I want to stay in this job, then I need to take care of myself. It took a while to talk myself into it, but I finally asked my supervisor for permission to take a self-care day today. She approved without giving it a second thought.

Waking up this morning, I feel a sense of calm wash over me. It feels good to be taking a day for myself and not focusing on anyone else. It feels good to be able to walk around my house freely without any fear. Of course, Billy following me around everywhere definitely helps.

After sitting on the couch watching TV for a while, it's almost time for lunch. I decide to use the bathroom first, then I'll figure out a food plan. Right after using the bathroom, I'm about to walk out when I hear a noise. It sounds almost like a knocking noise. I analyze the situation and at first, I can think logically. "Well, it sounds like it's coming from the master bathroom since that's on the other side of this bathroom. I'll just walk in and check it out."

Walking to the other room, things still feel okay. I still feel calm and proud of myself for handling this situation better than I would have before treatment. I don't see anything in the master bedroom, so I step into the master bathroom. Suddenly the thoughts start, and I no longer have control.

Thought Log:

Someone is upstairs and those are footsteps. They're here to rape you then kill you.

It's time to put my protection plan in place. Lock the bathroom door, call Cody and be ready to go out the window if someone gets in the bathroom. If I can I'll help Billy out the window, so he's not stuck inside with the killer. I think about calling 911, but I don't know if it's just my OCD or if it's happening. I sit in the fetal position on the shower rug, waiting for Cody to answer the phone. Only tears and panic come out as I try to speak, "I thi… I think someone is in… the house."

"Where are you? Are you okay? I'm coming home right now." I can hear Cody climbing into his truck.

"I'm in the bathroom with the door locked. I heard a sound, so I came to check it out and it sounded like someone was coming through the window upstairs! Cody, it's happening. Someone is going to get me, and I won't be able to do anything!"

"It's okay. I'm coming home." I shut my eyes while Billy starts growling and barking at the sound.

Thought Log:

They're going to kill you while you're on the phone, so Cody has to hear everything.

"Billy is barking at the noise now. It's not just me hearing it." It's getting more and more real by the second.

Thought Log:

They're going to kill Billy and make you watch. You caused this to happen.

"He sees you're scared and wants to protect you. I checked the cameras and they're clear. I don't see anyone coming in or out. I'll be there in twenty minutes, I promise. When I get there, stay in the bathroom while I check the house." His voice is shaking. I've never heard him sound like this before. He's scared.

"Please be careful and don't get pulled over." I know Cody and I know if he gets pulled over when I'm in danger, there's no chance he'll pull over. He'll lead the cops to the house and likely get arrested when he gets here.

"I know, I'll be okay."

I can't let something happen to him. The killer inside the house can come get me but needs to leave Cody alone. "When you get here, come through the screen door but leave it open so you can run out if you need to."

"I'm not going to leave you inside if someone is in the house!" Cody practically yells at me.

"I don't want you to be hurt if someone is here. What if they hurt you? I couldn't live with that!" I think for a minute and know what I need to do. "I want to call the police."

"Do what you need. I'll be there soon." I can hear the fear in his voice as he says, "I love you baby."

"I love you too." My heart breaks. I know they'll be the last words I'll ever say to my husband. I have no hope of making it out of the bathroom alive. My time is up. I am about to be killed and there is nothing I can do to stop it. Every fear I have ever felt is coming true.

While dialing 911, the sound continues. "911, what's your emergency?"

"Hi, I think someone is in my house. I'm locked in the bathroom right now."

"Okay, what's the address?" I give her my address but can barely focus on what she's saying. My eyes are on the doorknob, waiting for it to turn. The killer will find me soon. "Ma'am, what are the sounds?"

"They sound like footsteps! My dog is growling because he can hear them too." Worry grows that she doesn't believe me. Maybe since Billy is hearing them too, she's more likely to believe me.

"Does it sound like there's some type of animal in the walls or running around the house?"

"I don't know, I don't think so," but really, I'm already doubting myself. I know it's likely something other than a person, but I can't admit it. If I admit it, then that solidifies the fact that I lost to the OCD.

I hear a car door shut so I look out the bathroom window. A cop is walking up to the house from the driveway. I knock on the window so he can see where I am. I hear him enter the house through the only unlocked door. He starts to yell to identify himself. I'm waiting for the gunfire to start between the cop and killer. When I don't hear anything, I yell. "I'm in here!" Eventually, I open the bathroom door fearful that the officer is somehow in on the break in.

Thought Log:

You should've gone out the window. You shouldn't have left the bathroom. You're unsafe now and they're going to get you. No one can protect you.

"What's going on ma'am?" the cop asks.

I'm hyperventilating while trying to tell him what happened. "There are sounds of footsteps upstairs, so I locked myself in the bathroom. My husband is on his way home, but he couldn't get here fast enough, and I was worried he'd be hurt if he got here, and someone was in the house." The cop pulls out his gun and makes his way upstairs. Seeing a weapon out makes it more real. Part of me hopes he'll find something, so I don't sound crazy. I can't help but think "Please be real and not all in my head."

I'm standing at the bottom of the stairs, unsure what to do with myself. Should I run outside in case something happens upstairs? What if the killer runs down before the cop and still manages to kill me? Right as I'm contemplating what to do, a second cop walks inside the house to tell me everything is clear outside. After taking a quick look at the doors and checking the locks, he asks all the same questions as the first cop. "Did you hear anyone run down the stairs? Did you hear someone try to open any doors?" I don't know! I can't think clearly anymore. Tears are still falling, and my breathing is far from normal.

The first cop comes back down the stairs to tell me there's no one inside, and no signs anyone has even attempted to do so. I briefly think about telling them that I have OCD so sometimes this happens, but will they even understand how OCD can cause this? What if they try to hospitalize me? How will I ever recover if they try to put me away?

Right when the cops are about to leave, Cody makes it home. I'm standing next to the cops with my head down, while they tell Cody that everything's clear. They instruct him to call back if something turns up missing. After they leave, Cody comes towards me, wraps me up in his arms and leads me to the couch. "Do you want to tell me what happened?"

All I can get out are cries. I've been defeated. There's no reason to fight against it anymore. My OCD has won. I start rocking back and forth when the sound starts again. I cover my ears, drop my head to my knees and scream, "MAKE IT STOP!" The sound isn't real, and I know that now, but that doesn't stop my thoughts from telling me I am about to be killed. It still feels like someone is upstairs and I have no hope of being saved.

I hear Cody tell me to stand up so we can go outside. "I hear it too and I'm going to figure out what it is."

"Please don't leave me! It's not safe!" I sit down on the deck, leaning on the house in the fetal position. It feels like all the progress I had made was just thrown out the window. I let OCD take over. I'm a failure.

"I think the sound is the construction equipment out here that's rattling the house" Cody is looking around, doing all he can to find the source of the sound.

"When we were inside, did it sound like footsteps to you?" I asked, holding onto hope, that my reaction was normal.

"To me it sounded like it came from outside, but I can understand how you thought it was footsteps. I'm still going to walk through the house and crawl through the attic though to make sure there's no animals or anything." I appreciate his honesty and being sensitive to my fragile state, but I know nothing is in there. I know there is no point in checking the house, but even logic can't stop the thoughts.

Thought Log:

No matter how many times you check the house, someone will still be there, waiting for their time to attack. Just wait. You're not safe.

After a few more minutes of sitting outside, my breathing returns to normal. My face is covered in tears, and I'm covered in dried sweat. "I need to shower, but please don't leave me. I need you to stay with me because I can't be alone right now."

Thought Log:

The killer was upstairs and ran down to the bathroom while you were outside.

We make our way to the bathroom, but Cody does a quick check before I go in. While I'm in the shower, I make sure to talk with Cody to ensure he's still there. My sense of safety is little to none. More so, my emotional state is at an all-time low. I felt crazy before and now it's verified. I officially let it go too far and it's pathetic. I'm a mess that doesn't deserve treatment because it's obviously not working.

***

When I'm done showering, I feel relieved that Cody is still leaning against the sink, safe and sound. I tell him that I need to call Wanda. After I dry off and get dressed, Cody sits on the bed with me while I make the call. "Hey Wanda, um something bad happened. I was home alone and thought a noise was someone getting into the house. I ended up locking myself in the bathroom and calling the police. I don't think they believed me though and think I'm crazy now."

"Andrea, you must learn how to be okay with the unknown. You must be okay knowing that someday someone may be in the house," Wanda replies.

"That's hard to do. How am I ever supposed to feel safe?"

"Part of the process is learning how to feel safe in yourself and learning how not to check every time. Also, being okay that the police may not believe you. Now what are you going to do today to take care of yourself?"

"Well Cody is going to take me out to lunch since I never got to eat. Then I'll probably write a journal entry and take tomorrow off in order to give myself time to process what happened. Cody is going to take the day off too, so I don't have to be home alone again."

"That's a good plan. Let me know if you need anything else."

I hang up the phone feeling defeated but also proud of myself. I handled the situation the best I could in my current state of mind. I followed my gut and no one else was there to know what was going on. Plus, Cody is okay, which was one of my biggest fears when I first called him to help.

After doing another check-in, Cody starts to check the attic while I decide to journal to try to process what happened.

Journal Entry: Well today sucked. I thought I was being smart for taking the day off but instead I traumatized myself. Maybe it's okay because I took the right steps. I don't know if other people would have done the same thing, but I'm proud of myself. My biggest fear came true, or I thought it was coming true, and I got help. I'm smart and capable in those situations. I don't care right now if it was my OCD or not. This may be a setback, but it doesn't erase all the progress I had made. I can do it.

* * *

It's a few days after the incident and my mind is still out of sorts. It's been a while, but I decide to attend my support group. I've tried to talk with Cody, Wanda, Dre, Joy and Alex about all of this. They're all supportive and helpful, but there's something missing. I need more. I just don't know what it is yet. This support group is my last hope.

There's a big group today with six attendees, not counting the two facilitators. During the check-in portion, I bring up the break-in incident. When the facilitators ask if I want time to speak after check-ins, I don't hesitate. "Yes, I need to talk about it more. Heads up though it may be more venting than anything."

After some other attendees discuss what's going on with them, the facilitator looks towards me. "Alright Andrea, you're up as long as everyone is okay to move on." Looking around the table, everyone nods their heads and looks at me with supportive smiles.

After taking a deep breath, I start talking about what happened. By the end, I feel like I was just talking to myself rather than everyone else. It's like a way of processing. "The problem is, I don't know if I should be upset with myself, or proud of how I handled things. At first, I felt completely defeated. Like OCD had officially won the war inside my head. Then I started thinking about it more and thought maybe I should be proud of how I handled it. My worst nightmare came true, and I figured it out. I asked for help and got it, just like my plans always told me to do."

Silence takes over while it seems everyone is contemplating my story. One of the regular attendees speaks up. "It sounds like you should be proud of yourself. No one else had a clue what was happening, so you just followed your instincts. That's what you're supposed to do." It's the answer I'd been looking for.

I can't help but smile before my mind starts to get mixed up again. "That's what I've been wanting to feel, but it's been hard to validate that feeling. I feel like I messed up so bad by taking up the police's time. Then again, like you said, I didn't have a choice."

"Exactly. That's what the police are there for, to help people."

"Yeah, I know. I'm just really trying to keep moving forward. For a while, I wanted to stop trying my treatment. I didn't see any point because I knew I had already lost. Now, I'm just doing all I can to stay out of that mindset." Suddenly, I realize I'm talking about more than just this incident. "Actually, I think I just realized the positive things that came out of the dog attack." I pause while I connect the dots in my head.

"What positives are those?" Everyone is looking at me with interested eyes.

"Well, a lot of my treatment and progress happened after the dog attack. It sucked that it happened, and I hate that it happened. Honestly though, I'm not sure if I would have changed my mindset so much after it happened. I've learned how to speak up for my safety and take care of myself. Before that happened, I thought I was doing okay, but I clearly wasn't. I was doing a horrible job taking care of myself. I was pushing myself to a burnout, just like I did in the past." The realization happens. "The dog attack started it all." It feels like a weight is lifted off my chest. It all makes sense now. I can't continue to keep seeing these things in a negative light. My life has completely changed because of it. All I feel in this moment is relief. *I have OCD and that's okay. I got this.*

Conclusion

On December 10, 2019, my therapist told me I was officially in recovery from OCD. It was something I never thought was possible. In fact, I didn't even realize what she had told me until hours later. I remember looking it up online to see if recovery from a mental illness was even possible. I figured I had misheard what she said, but it was real! All the exposure therapy, support groups, therapy sessions, journaling, thought logs and crying sessions were worth it!

Unfortunately, just because I was placed in recovery, doesn't mean the negative thoughts went away completely. Three years later when I hear a noise in my house, my first thought still revolves around someone waiting to come kill me. The difference is that now, I can laugh it off and move on with my day. I'm finally at a place where I can say to myself 'someday someone may break into my house and try to hurt me and that's okay.'

* * *

Since my recovery, my husband and I welcomed a baby boy who is the light of our lives. Through my pregnancy I worked a lot in therapy on how to ensure I don't pass along my OCD tendencies to my son. Learning how to be okay with the unknown when it revolves around your child is a whole different level. I'm incredibly grateful I had time to learn about myself, develop coping strategies and determine my values before we expanded our family.

The most important value when we were welcoming our son was that I wanted to be present. For so long I was wrapped up in fear, I didn't want that anymore for myself, Cody or our son. Most of my childhood memories revolve around obsessions and compulsions. I want to replace those memories with ones of my son playing, learning new things and being the daredevil that he's growing up to be. I've taken thousands of pictures and videos so when he gets older, I'll always be able to remember. When the days are moving fast and I'm wrapped up in other things, he always seems to know when we need to take a little time to hang out. One morning, after a week of stressful mornings, he didn't want to leave the house because he wanted Cheerios. Even though it was going to make us late, I realized he was right. Sometimes we just need to stop to eat some Cheerios. We laughed while making funny faces at each other. He fed me Cheerios from his gross slobbery hands. Moments like those remind me why I went through all the pain of treatment. If I had a child in the depths of my OCD, I would never be able to be present like I'm able to be today.

After two and a half years in recovery, on June 17, 2022, my therapist told me I no longer meet criteria for a diagnosis. After nearly twenty years, I've overcome my biggest battle. I can officially say that I am recovered.

www.ingramcontent.com/pod-product-compliance
Lightning Source LLC
Chambersburg PA
CBHW062109290426
44110CB00023B/2760